The Church in the Age of Hip Hop

By Reverend Joseph Saunders

Edited, Designed, and Published by:

Desktop Prepress Services
Donna L. Ferrier
808 S. New Bethel Blvd.
Ada, OK 74820
1-866-220-4160
http://www.desktopprepress.com

Front and back cover images and inside graphics © 2009 by Jupiter Images.

Scripture taken from the King James Version of the Holy Bible.

Scripture taken from the HOLY BIBLE, NEW INTERNATIONAL VERSION® ©1973, 1978, and 1984 by International Bible Society. Used by permission of Zondervan. All rights reserved.

Scripture quotations taken from the Amplified® Bible, Copyright © 1954, 1958, 1962, 1964, 1965, 1987 by The Lockman Foundation. Used by permission. (www.Lockman.org)

Printed in the United States of America.

ISBN 978-0-578-01448-7

Table of Contents

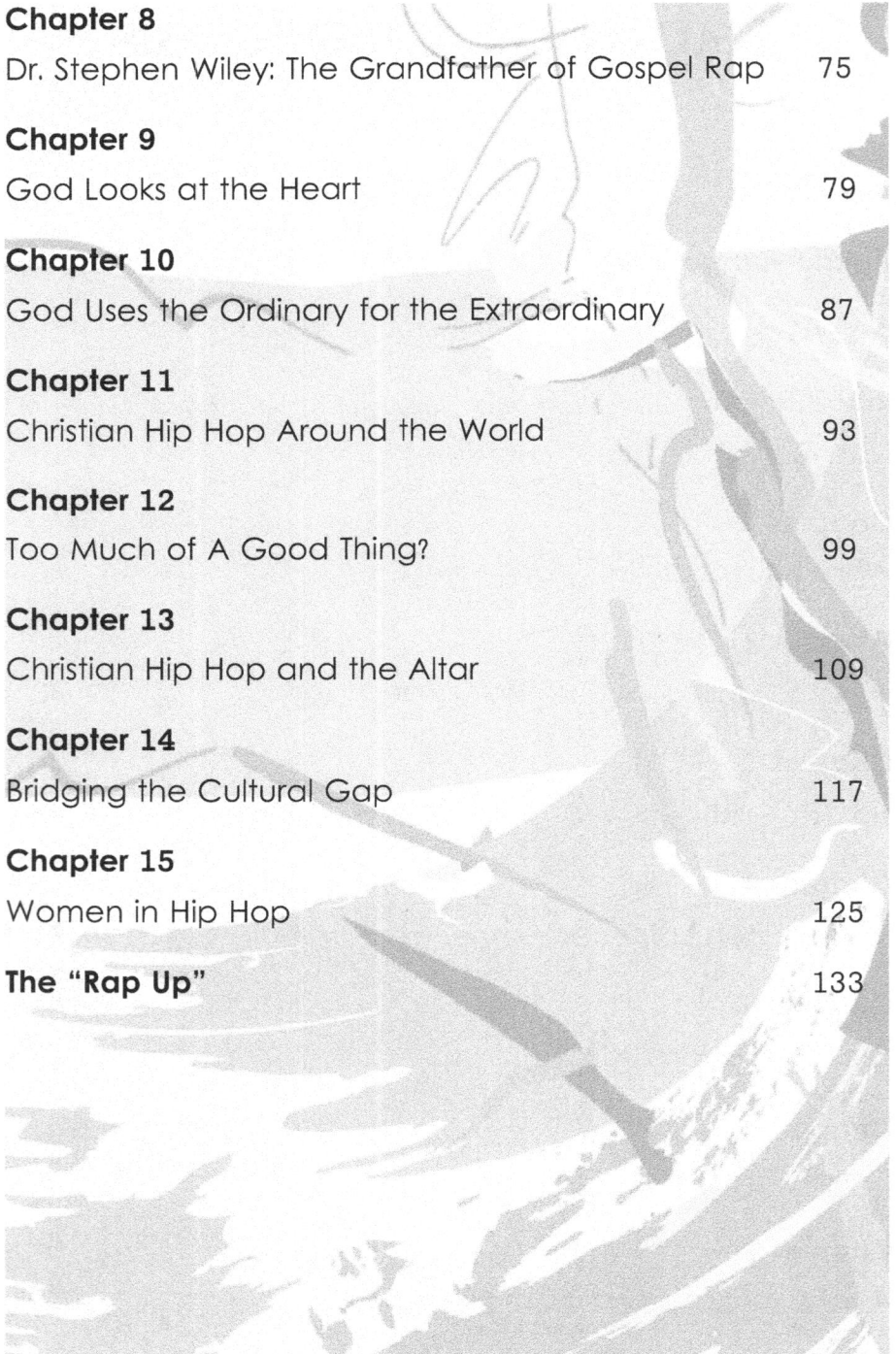

Dedication

This book is humbly dedicated to my father, Dr. Clinton H. Saunders, Jr., and my mother, Avis Avcn Saunders.

Acknowledgements

Above all, I would like to thank God for allowing me to write this book.

I would also like to thank my grandfather Clinton H. Saunders Sr who is now with the Lord. Both he and my grandmother pointed me to salvation. Thank you, Grandma, for telling me about Jesus in such a great way that I accepted Him into my life at age 14.

I would also like to thank my other grandmother, Erma Hilliard, and my other grandfather, Oliver Hillard, who has also gone to glory.

I would also like to thank my wife, Tara L. Saunders, for supporting me in all my works. Thank you for being a good Christian wife.

Also, thanks go to to my mother Avis Saunders for showing so much love for me in the everything thing that I do. I am so grateful to have such a great hardworking mom who showed me that if you keep working hard you will always have the things that you need. Thanks also to my dad, Dr. Clinton H. Saunders, Jr., who has been there for me through thick and thin. He showed me and continues to show me the true meaning of being a real Christian man.

I would like to thank my stepmother, who I really do not like to call, "step" because she has been a very strong influ-ence in my life. Both she and my biological mom are strong Christian women, and someday when we are all in heaven together, we will be one big heavenly family. There will be no "biological this" or "step that" because we will all be one under Jesus. It is so good to know
that there is no separation in heaven, and that our goal here on earth is to reflect just a taste of what our life will be like with Jesus.

Thanks also go to my brother Clinton L. Saunders (aka Shamel Shiloh) for who he is and everything he is doing for the kingdom of God. Out of all the rappers in the world, past and present, he is my favorite. When we were both in the world, you were my best rapper, and now that we are both serving the Lord full time, you are my best rapper once again.

Thanks so much to Tawanna Saunders for being a good wife to my brother.

And thanks also to my other brother, Napoleon. Remember

that the express still moves.

Thanks also to my sister, Juanita. People always say that you and I look just alike and have the same kind of humor. The world must really be blessed to have two of a kind.

Thank you, Tammy, for being a wonderful sister.

Thank you, too, Shauntrell, and remember to always keep Jesus first in your heart. You are a wonderful baby sister, as well.

And thank you, Savetreia, for not only being my big sister, but also being my sister in the gospel ministry.

I would also like to thank my cousin, Danetta, for being a strong supporter of the family. Josephine and I were once talking about how you should win best supporting family member if someone ever decided to give out awards for family support. You have supported not only me and Lamont, but the entire family from young to old. Again I cannot thank you enough.

I'd like to thank Uncle Ira for being good to my aunt and a good Christian. I'd also like to thank my aunt Lutricia for listening to my long stories even when she was tired.

And thanks to my aunt, Doll, who has always been there for me even when I was down at times. Thank you Uncle Joe for keeping grandma and being there for her. May the Lord continually richly bless you.

I'd also like to thank all my my nieces and nephews: Shakeya, Anita, Shenita, Shamel, Tysheera, Tiquan, McKenzie, Joseph jr, Antony, Jeremiah, and I cannot forget about my cousins: Chris, Jamal, Tiffany and Daniel.

I'd also like to thank the entire Mount Victory Baptist family, as well as Reverend Darrell and Tammy Prather, Reverend Julia Woodhouse, Evangelist Morgan, Reverend Johnny and Christina Saxton, and Reverend Vincent and Savetria Palmer. And special thanks to Pastor Marcus E. Turner and his wife Lisa Turner. Thank you for all of your support through the years. May God continue to guide you and your wife with His wisdom.

Thanks also to Pastor Buckner and his wife Avis, and Pastor Jones of Parkview Baptist church.

Thanks also to my aunt, Reverend Hilliard, and my uncle Frenchie.

Thanks also to the Gates family, Reverend Trammel and his family, Pastor Charles Bowen, Pastor Baker, Dr. Jones, Steve, and the 705th MP Battalion, 2nd Engineer Battalion.

Last but not least, thanks to my editor, Donna L. Ferrier, of Desktop Prepress Services, who has edited and published both of my books.

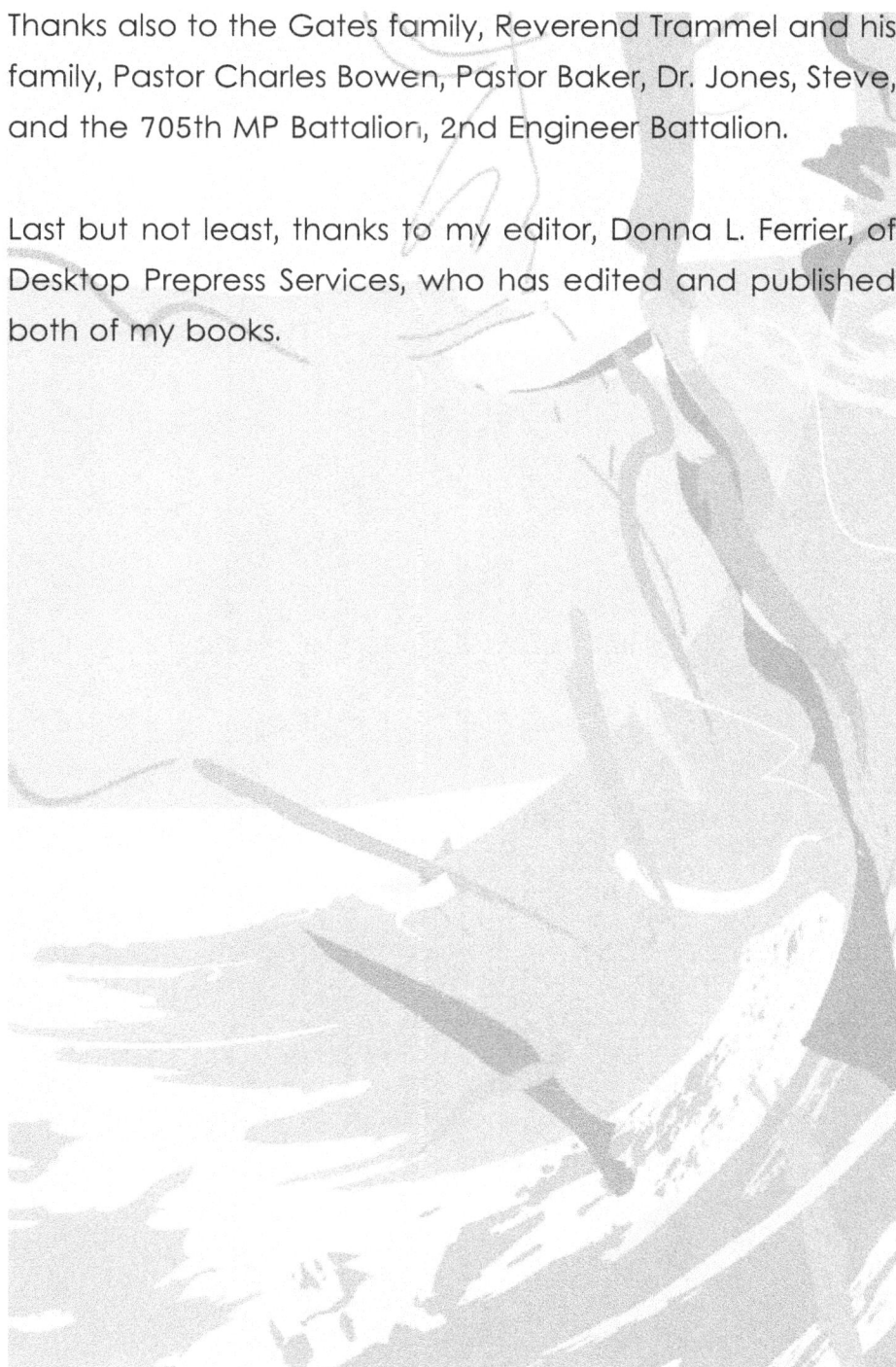

Foreword

By Rev. Dr.Clinton H. Saunders

T his is a great opportunity for me to comment on the new area of Christian music. I am talking about Christian Hip Hop. Although this form of music has been around for a while, the traditional faith based establishments are slow to accept this music. I was introduced to the music through my sons. One of them was a rapper and the other son was a producer. Anything that my sons are involved in, I like to be informed. The name Christian Hip Hop threw me off at first. But there is one thing I have learned n life, and that is don't jump to conclusions without facts.

When I noticed that my sons were heavily involved in Christian Hip Hop, it was time for me to investigate. I listened to the words of their music and discovered that they were doctrinal and biblically correct. Also the rhythms and the beat of the music were drawing people who would have otherwise never heard the message of Jesus Christ. Christian Hip Hop is a great evangelistic tool, and I am very grateful for you, Joseph, for writing about this genre of music.

I will conclude with this fact. There was a young lady, years ago who was a phenomenonal gospel singer, but was told that her style of singing was too jazzy. I am glad that this young lady did not allow criticism to stand in her way. The singer was Mahalia Jackson. She is now the standard by which gospel singers are judged.

The situation with Christian Hip Hop reminds me of the same situation as Mahilia Jackson. As long as there are young people who are not afraid to push the envelope and venture into new areas of proclaiming the gospel, God's message will be declared to every generation. This book will give others who do not understand a message that Christian Hip Hop reaches the masses. Isn't this what God commanded us to do? We need to encourage those who are part of the Christian Hip Hop community because young people are being saved through this music. Thanks again for this book. This is needed and I support you.

--- Rev. Dr. Clinton H. Saunders

Introduction
Can God Use Hip-Hop?

C hristian hip-hop has been under a lot of scrutiny lately. The saved and the unsaved alike are continually wondering, "Can God use Christian hip-hop for his purpose?" One of the main reasons for this dilemma lies in how people define the term, "Christian hip-hop." In order to arrive at an appropriate definition, we need to look at God's Word because even though Christian hip-hop is obviously a more recent development than the inspirational writing of the scriptures, Jesus Christ is the same yesterday, today, and forever, and so is His Word:

Isaiah 40:8: "The grass withers and the flowers fall, but the word of our God stands forever."

Hebrews 13:8: "Jesus Christ is the same yesterday and

today and forever."

It's safe to say that God can and does use Christian hip-hop because God has always used culture for His purposes throughout scripture, and that's precisely what Christian hip-hop is: a subculture within the American culture. So to say that God cannot use Christian hip-hop is to limit His Word, whether intentionally or unintentionally. Ironically, much of the culture that God used for His purpose throughout history has been evil, idolatrous, and entirely unholy culture. So, the bottom line is: if God can use evil for his purpose, can't He use the saints as well, even if they're not listening to organ music?

Let's take a look at some examples of the unholy cultures that God has used in the Old Testament to accomplish His purposes for His people, and then we'll look at how God uses culture in the New Testament. Joseph was under Egyptian culture in its fullest in Genesis 41:41. Pharaoh made him second in command of the entire land of Egypt, complete with the Pharaoh's signet ring, fine linen garments, and gold around his neck. God didn't say, "Joseph, if anything from the Egyptian culture is offered to you, don't take it." Rather, God said, "Joseph, I'm going to use this culture for my purpose." In the end, we see what that purpose was in Genesis 47: God used Joseph to save his people from the famine, including his very family who sold him into slavery in the first place!

Moses, the God-appointed leader for the Israelite Exodus, was raised entirely in the Egyptian culture after his basket was pulled out of the Nile by Pharaoh's daughter. And then when the Egyptian-raised Moses led the Israelites out of Egypt, God instructed Israel to take plunder of gold, silver, and clothing in Exodus 12:35-36 because He gave His Israelites victory over the idol-worshipping, hard-hearted Egyptians:

"The Israelites did as Moses instructed and asked the Egyptians for articles of silver and gold and for clothing. The LORD had made the Egyptians favorably disposed toward the people, and they gave them what they asked for; so they plundered the Egyptians."

There are many other places in the Old Testament that God uses the people and culture of the surrounding nations (who, by the way, were all idol worshippers) to care for the Israelites. In fact, Jeremiah 27:6-7 and 43:10-13 call Nebuchadnezzar king of Babylon "God's servant" because He used Nebuchadnezzar as an instrument of judgment upon the idol-worshipping nations:

"Then say to them, 'This is what the LORD Almighty, the God of Israel, says: I will send for my servant Nebuchadnezzar king of Babylon, and I will set his throne over these stones I have buried here; he will spread his royal canopy above them. He will come and attack Egypt, bringing death to those destined for death, captivity to those destined for captivity, and the sword to those destined for the sword. He will set fire to the temples of the gods of Egypt; he will burn their temples and take their gods captive. As a shepherd wraps his garment around him, so will he wrap Egypt around himself and depart from there unscathed. There in the temple of the sun in Egypt he will demolish the sacred pillars and will burn down the temples of the gods of Egypt.'"

It's important to note, however that Nebuchadnezzar wasn't God's servant because he worshipped God; rather it was because he was used by God for His purposes upon the lives of His people, the Israelites. Case in point: God doesn't just use the saints; He uses the idolaters, too. In fact, God continued to use Nebuchadnezzar to plunder Tyre, Moab, Ammon, Edom, and even Judah as prophesied by Jeremiah in chapter 27 because Judah had an entire record of idolatry as well. But verses 8–15 record God's words that any nation, including Judah, who does not serve the King of Babylon would perish, not because Nebuchadnezzar was a holy man, but because he was God's chosen instrument of judgment upon the sin of idolatry. In fact, Jeremiah 27 in its entirety describes what will happen to those who do not serve the King of Babylon: famine, plague, and death. Note particularly verses 8–15:

"'If, however, any nation or kingdom will not serve Nebuchadnezzar king of Babylon or bow its neck under his yoke, I will punish that nation with the sword, famine and plague, declares the LORD, until I destroy it by his hand. So do not listen to your prophe-s, your diviners, your interpreters of dreams, your mediums or your sorcerers who tell you, 'You will not serve the king of Babylon.' They prophesy lies to you that will only serve to remove you far from your lands; I will banish you and you will perish. But if any nation will bow its neck under the yoke of the king of Babylon and serve him, I will let that nation remain in its own land to till it and to live there, declares the LORD.'

I gave the same message to Zedekiah king of Judah. I said, "Bow your neck under the yoke of the king of Babylon; serve him and his people, and you will live. Why will you and your people die by the sword, famine and plague with which the LORD has threatened any nation that will not serve the king of Babylon? Do not listen to the words of the prophets who say to you, 'You will not serve the king of Babylon,' for they are prophesying lies to you. 'I have not sent them,' declares the LORD. 'They are prophesying lies in my name. Therefore, I will banish you and you will perish, both you and the prophets who prophesy to you.'"

Jeremiah did go on to foretell Babylon's judgment in chapters 50–51, because it was an idol worshipping nation, and Nebuchadnezzar was an idol-worshipping king. The point here again is that every nation, every culture can be used by the Lord, whether it's a God-fearing nation with

God-fearing people or not. But that does not mean, however, that God will not judge that nation for its own sins. In fact, God raised up the Persians (another pagan nation), who conquered Babylon, to restore the Israelites to their native land, which God said He would do at the appointed time in Jeremiah 27:22. The restoration of the Jews to their land and the beginning of the plans for building the second temple is recorded in Ezra 1:1-4:

"In the first year of Cyrus king of Persia, in order to fulfill the word of the LORD spoken by Jeremiah, the LORD moved the heart of Cyrus king of Persia to make a proclamation throughout his realm and to put it in writing: 'This is what Cyrus king of Persia says: The LORD, the God of heaven, has given me all the kingdoms of the earth and he has appointed me to build a temple for him at Jerusalem in Judah. Anyone of his people among you— may his God be with him, and let him go up to Jerusalem in Judah and build the temple of the LORD, the God of Israel, the God who is in Jerusalem. And the people of any place where survivors may now be living are to provide him with silver and gold, with goods and livestock, and with freewill offerings for the temple of God in Jerusalem.'"

Once again, note the phrase "the LORD, the God of heaven, has given me all the kingdoms of the earth and he has appointed me to build a temple for him at Jerusalem in Judah." God can and does use any culture to reach His people for whatever purpose He chooses.

When we get to the New Testament, our models for the idea that God uses culture are the Apostle Paul and our own Lord and Savior Jesus Christ Himself. Paul was a highly educated Pharisee according to Acts 23:6 and Philippians 3:5, a Roman citizen according to Acts 16:37–38, 22:27 and 29, and a Jew according to Acts 22:3 and 2 Corinthians 11:21–23. This enabled him to minister wherever the Holy Spirit sent him. He could also identify with the common people of the day because he was also a tentmaker according to Acts 18:3, so he knew what hard labor was. All this so that he could become "all things to all men" according to 1 Corinthians 9:22 so that he could lead people to Christ.

As for our Lord and Savior Jesus Christ, He was the best example of all of how God uses culture, and we can begin in Philippians 2:5–11:

"Your attitude should be the same as that of Christ Jesus: Who, being in very nature God, did not consider equality with God something to be grasped, but made himself nothing, taking the very nature of a servant, being made in human likeness. And being found in appearance as a man, he humbled himself and became obedient to death—even death on a cross! Therefore God exalted him to the highest place and gave him the name that is above every name, that at the name of Jesus every knee should bow, in heaven and on earth and under the earth, and every tongue confess that Jesus Christ is Lord, to the glory of God the Father."

Jesus' world is perfect; Heaven is perfect. But He, being the very nature of God Himself, laid aside His own nature to come down here to earth to meet man in his own world and culture, to become sin even though He was sinless (2 Corinthians 5:21), to become a servant made in human likeness, and to submit Himself to death on a cross—a Roman form of execution! He was tempted in every way just as we are, so that He could identify with man to atone for our sins and become our High Priest (Hebrews 2:17–18 and chapter 10).

You see, here in the New Testament, God continually uses culture that His people are already familiar with in order to reach others because when we want people to come to know Christ, we have to be able to identify with them where they are. Jesus came down here so that He could identify with us. And while He was here, he spoke to people in parables that largely contained agricultural imagery that peasant Jews would have been familiar with so that He could introduce His kingdom here on earth and talk about His future kingdom when Satan is ultimately thrown into the Lake of Fire; all suffering, disease, and sin are eradicated; and God's Kingdom reigns eternally.

God is still using culture today to reach the masses, just as Christ used the Jewish culture back in the first century to reach the Jews. And today, Christian hip-hop is one cultural venue Christ is using. Unfortunately, many say that God cannot use Christian hip-hop because they equate it with strip clubs and drug dealing. But 1 Corinthians 10:21 teaches us that we cannot drink of the cup of the Lord and the cup of demons at the same time. "Holy stripping" or "holy drug dealing," therefore, are oxymorons. And we are not "of the world" even though we do live "in it." And as long as we live in it, 1 John 2 15-16 commands believers not to partake in the world's sin:

"Do not love the world or anything in the world. If anyone loves the world, the love of the Father is not in him. For everything in the world—the cravings of sinful man, the lust of his eyes and the boasting of what he has and does—comes not from the Father but from the world."

Christians, in contrast to the world, are commanded to have a holy and pure ncture, which can only happen through Jesus Christ. Romans 12:2 says, "Do not conform any longer to the pattern cf this world, but be transformed by the renewing of your mind. Then you will be able to test and approve what God's will is—his good, pleasing and perfect will."

Strippers and drug dealers claiming to be Christians are false spirits, according to the verses just quoted. And Christians are commanded to test all spirits to see whether they are from God. 1 John 4:1 says, "Dear friends, do not believe every spirit, but test the spirits to see whether they are from God, because many false prophets have gone out into the world."

Unfortunately, many Christians today believe that every spirit who says he or she is from God actually is. But here are the keys to figuring it out: Are they exhibiting a transformed life and a transformed way of thinking according to Romans 12:2? Are they "new creations" in Christ, according to 2 Corinthians 5:17? If so, then those are true spirits from the Lord. And if the spirits are listening to Christian music with lyrics that are true to the Word of God, then what does it matter whether it's piano and violins or electric guitars and drums?

Jesus Himself said in Mark 9:23 that all things are possible for those who believe. So, the bottom line is do you believe that God can use Christian hip-hop, not to partake in stripping and drug dealing, but to identify with and bring to Christ those who do so that they can experience the transformed victorious life? If you can't quite "get there" yet, then test the spirits for yourself. Have you seen people come to Christ because of the music they listen to, even if it's not particularly in your taste? Remember, the question is not whether you listen to it, but whether God can use it.

Chapter 1
What Is Christian
Hip Hop?

C hristian hip hop is comprised of four main elements: Emceeing, also known as rapping; DJ-
ing; graffiti writing; and break dancing.
Rapping can be defined as feelings and in-
sights in the soul that are transformed into a verbal rhythmic
art form.

DJ-ing can be defined cs the groundwork of rapping. It
compliments the MC by adding sounds using two turntables
with two different persona ities working together for one
cause. At the same time, the listener hears a continuous
sound along with the turntables in play. Practically speaking,
we can liken DJ-ing to the deacon who compliments the

preacher while he is preaching or to the music that accompanies the altar call, tithes and offering, welcoming, benediction, or even when the preacher arrives at a particularly high moment in the sermon.

Graffiti writing can be defined as feelings and insights in the soul expressed visually. This form of expression is almost unshakable not only because of the strong imagery used in the drawings, but also because it's hard to remove. In the Christian world, Graffiti writing can be seen as evangelizing. In the secular world, graffiti artists spray paint on walls, subways, and government buildings, which is illegal, and it's never okay to vandalize public property. But just as these artists are willing to go to such extraordinary lengths to have their message be viewed, we need to go to equally extraordinary lengths to preach the gospel in places where it is still considered illegal to talk about Jesus. We need to fulfill the Great Commission of preaching the gospel to the ends of the earth (Acts 1:8).

Sadly enough, there are still so many places where the gospel is illegal. Many foreign countries throw people in jail, burn their homes down, or even execute them just because they're Christians. Even here in the United States of America, children can be thrown out of school for praying, and yet they can go to school with green hair, 100 body piercings, or half naked. Gay and lesbian clubs are being started in our school systems now, but yet we can't talk about

Christ. Preachers can be thrown in jail in Canada for preaching against homosexuality, even though both the Old and New Testaments clearly teach that homosexuality is a sin, because that's considered a hate crime.

At any rate, when we speak of graffiti as evangelism, we can think about wearing Christian t-shirts, for example, or sporting Christian bumper stickers or jewelry---something that doesn't constitute breaking the law that shows our spirituality on the outside. True Christian graffiti, however, is the Word of God engraved and living in a person's heart for the whole world to see every time the Christian opens his or her mouth and lets that Holy Spirit just flow right out of his or her being, as He radiates the whole person. This kind of graffiti can never be removed.

And last but not least, break dancing is feelings and insights in the soul expressed nonverbally through body movement. When we speak in a Christian context, break dancing can be seen as an act of praise. Even King David danced in a linen ephod after God used him and the entire house of Israel to rescue the Ark of the Covenant from the house of Obed-Edom and bring it home to the City of David, with shouts and the sound of trumpets, even though David's wife (who was a daughter of Saul, by the way) thought he was disgracing himself. When Christians do a praise dance they do it for the glory of God in view of many, not for show, but as an act of worship.

Together, these four elements comprise the hip hop culture. Understanding these various elements has given me personally a greater understanding of how God works through them. He uses the rapping to communicate His Word to the masses through the rapper's rhythmic art form. That doesn't necessarily mean that the rapper is always rapping scripture straight from the Bible, but as long as his or her message lines up with scripture, it is not sin. After all, Jesus used parables throughout the gospels to teach earthly principles that pointed to a heavenly meaning.

There are also spin-off elements from Christian hip hop that complement the original four, such as beat boxing, hip hop fashion, and slang. Beat boxing is simply making creative sounds with the mouth, lips, tongue, and voice to constitute an art form. In Christianity, we can think of beat boxing as making a joyful noise unto the Lord. God likes us to be creative when giving Him glory and honor, and making a joyful noise does not always have to constitute traditional singing and organ playing. A noise, whatever kind of noise it is, is always joyful if it glorifies God. And just like King David's dance that didn't yield approval from his wife, making a joyful noise does not have to win the approval of man—only God.

Hip hop fashion was a style of dress that came out of the inner city of the Bronx, New York. Now that hip hop has spread worldwide, it is no longer just in the Bronx but all over the world, and as popular culture changes, so does the hip hop style.

Hip hop fashion can defined more in a spiritual context rather than just clothes. My father, Dr. Clinton H. Saunders, Jr., preached a sermon one time from Zachariah, entitled, "Change Clothes." When the devil accused Zachariah, who stood in dirty clothes before God, Zachariah then put on his new garments, which represented his new nature, which can be cross referenced with 2 Corinthians 5:17: "Therefore, if anyone is in Christ, he is a new creation; the old has gone, the new has come!"

These garments represented three keys in the New Testament:

1) the a priestly robe (signifying his priesthood)

2) the king's crown (signifying his kingship), and

3) his office of prophet

No one else in the Old Testament fulfilled all three offices of prophet, priest, and king. Here in the New Testament, Jesus has fulfilled all three offices. He is our High Priest, which is talked about in the book of Hebrews. The priestly garments throughout the Bible set the priests apart from the rest of the people for the work of God in the temple. When we as Christians today live for Christ, our light should shine to the point where people see the difference from the inside, and not the outside. Matthew 5:15-17 says:

"Neither do people light a lamp and put it under a bowl.

Instead they put it on its stand, and it gives light to everyone in the house. In the same way, let your light shine before men, that they may see your good deeds and praise your Father in heaven."

That is not to say that we shouldn't care about our outward appearances, but Christian fashion means living life in line with the Word of God. 1 Timothy 2:8-10 says:

"I want men everywhere to lift up holy hands in prayer, without anger or disputing. I also want women to dress modestly, with decency and propriety, not with braided hair or gold or pearls or expensive clothes, but with good deeds, appropriate for women who profess to worship God."

The point of this passage was not to tell women what to wear to church, but that both men and women should be known for their Godly practices and lifestyles, not what they wear. Timothy wanted the actions and appearances of both genders to point toward the Lord, not to draw attention to themselves. True fashion is living a righteous life.

Slang is an endless list of terms that can be defined as an original cultural language that can be understood by the masses when properly applied. In Christian terms, it simply means having a new talk with Christ. When God has delivered us from a life of bondage, we will not speak the same way we did when we were still bound. When we are set free, we can talk about the things of the Lord without being ashamed. Consider the following verses:

Romans 1:16: "I am not ashamed of the gospel, because it is the power of God for the salvation of everyone who believes: first for the Jew, then for the Gentile."

2 Corinthians 10:8: "For even if I boast somewhat freely about the authority the Lord gave us for building you up rather than pulling you down, I will not be ashamed of it."

Philippians 1:20: "I eagerly expect and hope that I will in no way be ashamed, but will have sufficient courage so that now as always Christ will be exalted in my body, whether by life or by death."

2 Timothy 1:8: "So do not be ashamed to testify about our Lord, or ashamed of me his prisoner. But join with me in suffering for the gospel, by the power of God,"

2 Timothy 1:12: "That is why I am suffering as I am. Yet I am not ashamed, because I know whom I have believed, and am convinced that he is able to guard what I have entrusted to him for that day."

2 Timothy 2:15: "Do your best to present yourself to God as one approved, a workman who does not need to be ashamed and who correctly handles the word of truth."

Hip hop talk is nothing more than speaking freely about what God has done for us as a new creature of Christ. And along with the other elements of Christian hip hop I just discussed, it is a valuable tool for spreading the gospel. With all these elements of hip hop, we can combat false doctrine, lead people to Christ, fellowship, sing out praises to our Lord, and the list goes on. So, let's let God work, ok?

Chapter 2
A House United or a
House Divided?

One of the many problems the Christian hip-hop culture faces is an unwillingness in the church to come together as one family united in Christ and stay focused on Jesus. Christians and non-Christians alike see Christian hip-hop participants as unregenerate sinners. But the truth is there is nothing in scripture that teaches us what genre of Christian music to listen to, whether it be traditional or contemporary.

Granted we should be careful about what we place before our senses because the television programs we watch and the music we listen to go directly into the hearts of our bodies as the temples of the Holy Spirit. Psalm 101:3

says, "I will set before my eyes no vile thing. The deeds of faithless men I hate; they will not cling to me." And yes, even so-called Christian music can contain lyrics that are contrary to scripture. But style of music is solely a preference and not worthy of division because there's no way to prove in scripture that one style of Christian music is sinful and another isn't if the lyrics are scripturally sound.

The best way to decide for yourself whether Christian hip-hop participants are unregenerate sinners is to measure their character and activities against scripture. The same can be said for anyone, no matter what kind of music they listen to. The apostle Paul spends an inordinate amount of time in Romans 5 and 6 discussing the difference between people who don't know Christ and people who do.

First we need to figure out what it means to be regenerated in Christ, and for that we can turn to Romans 5:1, which shows that those who have been "justified through faith" in Christ, who have received the grace Jesus bestowed us on the cross while we were yet sinners, will have peace with God, which is ultimately reflected in how we live our lives. Do you see this God-given peace in the lives of Christian hip-hop participants? Do you sense the power of the Holy Spirit in their lives?

Verses 2-5 teaches that those who have been regenerated through faith in Christ will not only simply deal with their sufferings, but actually rejoice in them, because they know that "suffering produces perseverance; perseverance, character; and character, hope. And hope does not disappoint us, because God has poured out his love into our hearts by the Holy Spirit, whom he has given us." This is the "peace that surpasses all understanding" described in Philippians 4:4-7:

"Rejoice in the Lord always. I will say it again: Rejoice! Let your gentleness be evident to all. The Lord is near. Do not be anxious about anything, but in everything, by prayer and petition, with thanksgiving, present your requests to God. And the peace of God, which transcends all understanding, will guard your hearts and your minds in Christ Jesus."

This is the picture of the mature Christian believer. So, do you see this kind of joy and peace in the lives of Christian hip-hop participants? If so, then why does it matter so much that they're not listening to "your kind" of music?

The rest of Romans 5 teaches the magnitude of our justification by faith in Christ, and ultimately asks, "Where do we stand with God?" The fact is, we have either been justified by our faith in Christ and received the regenerating power of the Holy Spirit, or we are still in an unregenerate state under the penalty of sin. If we have received Christ, then our sin debt has been canceled and we can now begin living the righteous lives described in Romans 6, where Paul makes clear that we can only serve one master:

sin or righteousness. It's not a question of whether we will serve one, but rather a question of which one we will serve. This is called sanctification, and it simply means being set apart to serve God so that we can stop living under the power of sin and start living under the power of righteousness and holiness. Being set apart is something we mature in daily; it's a process of continually confessing the sins that we commit daily and letting Jesus remove those sins from our lives so that we can live more pure, more holy lives.

Another way to discern whether a person is living a righteous life is whether that person is obeying the Word of God. Ephesians 5:1 commands us, "Be imitators of God, therefore, as dearly loved children." 1 John 3:10 tells us how to discern between children of God and children of the devil: "This is how we know who the children of God are and who the children of the devil are: Anyone who does not do what is right is not a child of God; nor is anyone who does not love his brother." And finally John 14:23–24 says, "Jesus replied, 'If anyone loves me, he will obey my teaching. My Father will love him, and we will come to him and make our home with him. He who does not love me will not obey my teaching. These words you hear are not my own; they belong to the Father who sent me.'"

Sin has nothing to do with the style of Christian music we listen to; it has to do with not obeying the Word of God, and that's true in any area of Christian ministry. If, for ex-

ample, a man is called to full-time preaching and he does-
n't obey that calling, that man is in sin. And unless that person obeys his calling, he will put a barrier in his fellowship
with God as long as he's living in disobedience. James 4:17
says, "Anyone, then, who knows the good he ought to do
and doesn't do it, sins."

And finally, one who is obeying the Word of God will see
the fruits of the Spirit manifest in his or her life, and these
fruits will be seen by the masses. Galatians 5:22-23 defines
what the fruits of the Spirit are: "But the fruit of the Spirit is
love, joy, peace, patience, kindness, goodness, faithfulness,
gentleness and self-control. Against such things there is no
law."

By contrast Matthew 7:14-18 warns that false prophets
will bear bad fruit (which is how we know they are false):
"Watch out for false prophets. They come to you in sheep's
clothing, but inwardly they are ferocious wolves. By their fruit
you will recognize them. Do people pick grapes from thorn-
bushes, or figs from thistles? Likewise every good tree bears
good fruit, but a bad tree bears bad fruit. A good tree cannot bear bad fruit, and a bad tree cannot bear good fruit."

One thing to note about false prophets is that they do
everything in secret (hence the term "wolves in sheep's
clothing"). If they weren't false, they wouldn't have to wear
a spiritual disguise; they'd act out in the open. This is signif-
icant because Christian hip-hop artists are not afraid to

proclaim Christ right out in the open for everyone to see and hear.

To see some examples of bad fruit, we can turn back to Galatians 5: 19-21:

"The acts of the sinful nature are obvious: sexual immorality, impurity and debauchery; idolatry and witchcraft; hatred, discord, jealousy, fits of rage, selfish ambition, dissensions, factions and envy; drunkenness, orgies, and the like. I warn you, as I did before, that those who live like this will not inherit the kingdom of God."

Discord, dissensions, and factions are precisely what Paul was preaching against in 1 Corinthians 3:3-5, which is addressed to "mere infants in Christ," (1 Corinthians 3:1) when he said:

"You are still worldly. For since there is jealousy and quarreling among you, are you not worldly? Are you not acting like mere men? For when one says, "I follow Paul," and another, "I follow Apollos," are you not mere men?"

As long as the Christian music we listen to is scripturally sound, those who do not accept one type of Christian music or another are only serving to promote division, which is detrimental to the unity in the body of Christ. 1 Corinthians 12 describes very well how the body of Christ operates, so I encourage you to read that chapter thoroughly. Each of us is a part of the body, meant to function together as a unifying whole, with Christ as the head. When one part of the body is separated from the others, the body becomes unable to function in a healthy manner.

Ever think about physical body imagery in scripture? I think if we contemplated the image of the physical body more often and compared it with how the physical relates to the spiritual; we'd see a lot of truths we never saw before. Marriage, for example, is described as a one-flesh relationship in Genesis 2:24, but what happens when one flesh is ripped in two? Physically speaking, bones would break, blood vessels would be ripped to shreds, along with tendons, ligaments, tissue, etc. But that's a physical concept of what divorce is: one flesh ripped in two. That's precisely why divorce is so painful, physically and emotionally. It's both a physical as well as an emotional and spiritual death. The physical death is the divorce itself: the separation of the two people. And many times the emotional and spiritual death comes as a result. It's not irreparable, but it is crippling and painful.

Operating as a unifying "body of Christ" carries the same concept. If we're unified then we have all of our parts in place, but if one person breaks off from the body, it's like ripping off an arm or a leg and watching the blood gush everywhere. If this happened to a person physically, in all likelihood, that person would die. If not, that person would live the rest of his or her life physically impaired. Let's not cripple, or worse yet, kill ourselves, and Christ, all over again by breaking apart over superficial issues. Let's remember that we're all on the same mission of Matthew 28:19-20: "Therefore go and make disciples of all nations, baptizing them in the name of the Father and of the Son and of the Holy Spirit, and teaching them to obey everything I have commanded you."

Like all genuine, Spirit-filled Christians, Christian hip-hop artists believe that as long as people are breathing, they have a chance for redemption. And that's why they use their music to reach the secular hip-hop world. As discussed in chapter 1, using hip-hop with Christian lyrics gives unregenerate people who listen to the same kind of secular music something to identify with so that we can lead them to a personal relationship with Jesus Christ. And Romans 8:1 says that there is no condemnation for those who are in Christ Jesus. So if Jesus doesn't condemn Christians for listening to Christian music that may not be within our personal taste, then why should we?

One final point that should be addressed, however, is that some Christians may consider such music a "gray area" of Christianity, and that's ok because respecting people's "gray areas" serves to preserve unity in the body of Christ, as well. When church leaders talk about "gray areas," they are usually doing so in the context of Romans 14, so you can read that chapter for yourself. Even though I don't think listening to one form of Christian music or another means a person is spiritually weak or strong, verses 13–15 are particularly relevant to our discussion here:

"Therefore let us stop passing judgment on one another. Instead, make up your mind not to put any stumbling block or obstacle in your brother's way. As one who is in the Lord Jesus, I am fully convinced that no food is unclean in itself. But if anyone regards something as unclean, then for him it is unclean. If your brother is distressed because of what you eat, you are no longer acting in love. Do not by your eating destroy your brother for whom Christ died."

When applied to Christian music, one person simply may not be able to listen to certain styles of music, Christian or not. Someone might associate a certain form of music, or even a certain song, with a particular sin that person committed in the past. So, listening to that kind of music again, even when we put Christian lyrics to it, may cause that person to stumble because it could trigger an unpleasant or sinful past memory. So, we shouldn't force such believers to partake in activities that hurt them because we always want to make sure that we're always acting in love by not distressing our brothers and sisters in Christ.

Chapter 3
He Just Said, "Go"

When Jesus gave the Great Commission, He never told us how to go and make disciples of all nations; He just said "go." So, how will you proceed in the direction God is leading you? Paul tells us in Philippians 2:11–13 to work out our own salvation "with fear and trembling," and this is something that each of us has to do in our own lives. Paul doesn't spell out step by step how exactly we are to do this, but there are guidelines in scripture, beginning with the part of the verse I just quoted, "with fear and trembling." We are to take our walks with Christ seriously because of verse 13 that follows: "for it is God who works in you to will and to act according to his good purpose." We are to always keep in mind that whatever the great "I AM" leads us to do, He is the one who began the good work in us and He is the one who will be faithful to complete it (Philippians 1:6).

Three other wonderful scriptural guidelines to consider when working out our own salvations:

Proverbs 16:9: "In his heart a man plans his course, but the LORD determines his steps."

Proverbs 3:5-6: "Trust in the LORD with all your heart and lean not on your own understanding; in all your ways acknowledge him, and he will make your paths straight."

And, above all:

1 Corinthians 10:31: "So whether you eat or drink or whatever you do, do it all for the glory of God."

This is exactly what Christian hip-hop artists endeavor to do: take their walks seriously and wholeheartedly believe they are acting according to the work that God has given them. In other words, Jesus Christ Himself has led these brothers and sisters in Christ to produce their own unique style of Christian music to identify with the secular hip-hop world, which is full of lyrics about gangs, violence, sex, and drug addiction, in order to lead "gang bangers" into a world full of Christ's love and peace, teaching them to live lives holy and pleasing to the Lord.

We're not talking about compromising the Word of God; we're talking about using a style of music familiar to lost people in order to get them to repent and be saved and restored by Christ Jesus. And remember, a lot of these

Christian hip-hop artists came out of the drug and gang lifestyle themselves. Who better than to lead others out of it, too? This is exactly how God uses our painful memories of our past lives, to bring others in the same situations into a saving faith and a personal relationship with our Lord and Savior. Can Jesus use your past life to lead others to Him? How? Think about it.

Those of us who would condemn Christian hip-hop as "unholy" or as a "work of Satan" need to keep John 3:17 in mind: "For God did not send his Son into the world to condemn the world, but to save the world through him." Before we came to know the Lord, we all needed saving; we all needed Christ to forgive us of our sins and restore us into a right relationship with Him. God provided the way for this to happen: by sending His one and only Son to die on the cross for the sins of the world, and to save those who would turn from their sins and "receive God's abundant provision of grace," as stated in Romans 5:17. Once we are saved through faith in Christ's redeeming work on the cross and the power of the resurrection, we are to keep living by faith every moment of our lives, and this involves not only hearing Christ's words but putting them into practice.

In Matthew 7:24-27 Jesus likens the man who hears His words and does what He says to a wise man who build his house on rock. Verse 25 records the outcome: "The rain came down, the streams rose, and the winds blew and beat against that house; yet it did not fall, because it had its foundation on the rock." By contrast, verse 27 records the outcome of the foolish man who built his house on sand, representative of the man who does not obey the Word of God: "The rain came down, the streams rose, and the winds blew and beat against that house, and it fell with a great crash."

Other verses to keep in mind here are 1 John 3:10, which says that anyone who does not do what is right is not a child of God, Romans 14:23, which says that everything not done of faith is sin, and Hebrews 4:11, which is quoted from Psalm 95:7–8 commands, "Today, if you hear his voice, do not harden your hearts" in reference to the Jews who did not get into the promised land because of their disobedience to the Word of the Lord. And all Christian hip-hop artists are trying to do today is obey the message they've been given by the Lord so that their faith will strengthen and so they can lead other people to Christ.

You would be correct in saying that secular hip-hop has nothing to do with the gospel of peace because Christ is not the central theme of the music. And yes, there are Christian artists writing and performing secular hip-hop music, but those who live their lives this way are trying to drink from the cup of the Lord and the cup of demons at the same time, as recorded in 1 Corinthians 10:21, and live a life full of contradiction. In the end, Revelation 3:16 says that those who are "lukewarm" will be spit out of the Lord's mouth. People who try to straddle the Sword of the Spirit (i.e. the Word of God in Ephesians 6:17) will always get cut.

The bottom line is that no matter what kind of work the Lord gave us to do, fully trusting Christ and His Word is paramount. For when we reach the end of our lives, we want to hear Christ say, "Well done, good and faithful servant! You have been faithful with a few things; I will put you in charge of many things. Come and share your master's happiness!" (Matthew 25:21) The sincere desire of the Christian hip-hop artist, like many who are reading this book, is to hear those words, and live their lives with that goal in mind.

And in the end, God moves us all on to do other things. Many Christian hip-hop artists will not always be in that ministry (and yes it is a ministry) because when they have been faithful in their work, God will give them more to do. Ultimately, like many of us, they, too are striving to finish the race, which is ultimately as Paul describes it in Acts 20:24: "...If only I may finish the race and complete the task the Lord Jesus has given me—the task of testifying to the gospel of God's grace."

Note what Paul identifies as the ultimate goal of our lives as Christians, "testifying to the gospel of God's grace." And no matter who preaches the gospel of Christ, this gospel message will be spread. Paul says in Philippians 1:15, "It is true that some preach Christ out of envy and rivalry, but others out of goodwill." Whether they know it or not, all kinds of people have preached the gospel. Of course God-fearing faithful people have preached the gospel. Stephen, the first Christian martyr, is described in Acts 6:8 as, a man full of God's grace and power, did great wonders and miraculous signs among the people." Nonetheless, after he recounts all God had done for His people in Acts 7, he was stoned, but even as he was being tortured, he prayed for his captors: "Lord do not hold this sin against them" (Acts 7:60). Afterward, when the crowd scattered, so did the gospel.

Peter and John were flogged coming out of the synagogue for preaching the gospel, but would still rather obey God than man. Jesus Himself could have come off the cross instead of dying for our sins. He was God; He had the power to do it. Instead, however, He obeyed the will of His Father and defeated death.

But Paul also identified others who preached the gospel out of false motives in verse 17: "The former preach Christ out of selfish ambition, not sincerely, supposing that they can stir up trouble for me while I am in chains." But he continues in verse 18 by saying, "But what does it matter? The important thing is that in every way, whether from false motives or true, Christ is preached. And because of this I rejoice." Many unregenerate people preach the gospel and don't even know it. Anytime you hear a skeptic try to disprove Christianity, for example, guess what? Christ is being preached. Anytime you hear a drunk at a bar say to another drunk, "You need God," guess what? Christ is being preached. We come to know Christ because of the power of His gospel, not because we're all holy people.

Having said that, whether you believe that Christian hip-hop artists preach from false motives or true, guess what? Christ will always be preached. The gospel will always go forward. That doesn't mean that we shouldn't endeavor to live holy, blameless lives: like I've written here, that's exactly what the Christian hip-hop artist desires to do to advance the gospel, and to make sure it is preached correctly.

Having said all that, what is God leading you to do in your own life to advance the gospel? God uses us all in different ways, so what kind of work has He trusted you with? And what have you done with your Master's talents? Have you "gained five more" as in Matthew 25:16, or have you buried the one talent He gave you out of fear of losing it? Guess what? Operating out of fear only serves to make that fear come true, for Matthew 25:28 indicates that the one who hid his talent is the one who had it taken away. The object of every Christian hip-hop artist is to "gain five more." Are you living with that kind of contagious, life-giving faith, too?

Chapter 4
Being Mindful Of One Another

Christians need to be mindful of one another, as one body united in Christ. God calls us to love one another, not fight with one another. In fact, Proverbs 17:19 says, "He who loves a quarrel loves sin; he who builds a high gate invites destruction." And Proverbs 20:3 says, "It is to a man's honor to avoid strife, but every fool is quick to quarrel." In other words, scripture tells us vehemently to avoid quarrels and strive, not incite them. Paul told the new Corinthian believers in 1 Corinthians 3:3 that they were still worldly because there was still quarreling and strife among them. So, if we engage in quarreling and fighting, the best we can hope for is to be called "worldly Christians." Not a pretty picture, is it?

Most issues that Christians debate over have absolutely nothing to do with carrying out the Great Commission of Matthew 28:19-20: "...go and make disciples of all nations, baptizing them in the name of the Father and of the Son and of the Holy Spirit, and teaching them to obey every-thing I have commanded you...." Over the years, I have learned two things in my Christian walk: 1) Not to discuss Christian debates with the unsaved, and 2) Mature Chris-tians should be able to guide difficult situations that arise in the church to a mature close.

People who are mature in their walks with Christ are just as much sinners as people who aren't mature. Romans 3:23 says, "All have sinned and fall short of the glory of God." And the same God who justifies the mature Christian is the same God who justifies the babe in Christ. The difference is that those who are mature have let Christ crucify more of their flesh and have grown further in the process of sancti-fication than the babe in Christ has. Mature believers also understand more of the Word than immature believers. There are usually two reasons for believers being immature: 1) They have just come to know Christ and are still young in the Lord or 2) They are not growing in their walks and never get passed the "babe in Christ" stage. People who fall into the second category may have known the Lord for 20 years and are still immature because they have not stayed connected with the Lord through the Word, which is the primary tool for spiritual growth, and prayer, which is our communication with God.

I tell you, though, believers who have just come to know Christ have an awful lot of fire, and it is here that we have to remember the difference between the Corinthians and the Thessalonians. The Corinthian believers were young Christians only because they were engaging in the things of the world and were not growing in their walks and separating themselves from ungodly practices. The Thessalonians were young Christians who were growing rapidly in their faith into maturity. In fact, according to 1 Thessalonians 1:8: "The Lord's message rang out from you not only in Macedonia and Achaia—your faith in God has become known everywhere." We need to be more like the Thessalonians, engaged in maturing in our faith and letting God's message ring out everywhere!

One of Paul's main goals of Romans was to declare the playing field "leveled" between the Jews and the Greeks. The Jews thought that they were better than the Greeks because they were given a special covenant with the Lord that the Greeks didn't have, and the Greeks thought they were better for cultural reasons. But then Paul came along and told both groups that a) The Greeks were fools because they had fallen into idolatry, and therefore, the knowledge that they did have through God's creation had

become corrupt; b) The Jews were engaging in self-right-
eous judgment of the Greeks because the Jews were
doing the same things the Greeks were (after all, they did
have an entire Old Testament history of idolatry, which re-
sulted in exile and a divided kingdom, lest they forget); and
c) The same God who justifies the Jews also justifies the
Greeks: "those who receive God's abundant provision of
grace and of the gift of righteousness" will "reign in life
through the one man, Jesus Christ" (Romans 5:17). Make no
mistake: telling the covenantal Jews that they were no better than the idolatrous, sexually immoral Gentiles was be-
yond insulting. But the truth in Romans 3:23 is underscored:
"all have sinned and fall short of the glory of God."

So, if none of us are better than another, and if we all
commit the same sins, then why are we all looking down
on one another, especially because of something so trivial
as the style of music we listen to? So what if some of us like
traditional hymns, while others relate better to more contemporary worship? So what if some of us like organ music,
while others of us can relate to people doing back flips on
stage? Has everyone been called to the same ministry to
the same people? Can everyone relate to the same life experiences? Was everyone raised the same way? Of course
not.

The apostle Paul really did "become all things to all
men" He was a Jew, a Roman citizen, a Pharisee, and most

importantly, a strong Christian and one of the greatest evangelists in history. And as he says in 2 Corinthians 11:24–26:

"Five times I received from the Jews the forty lashes minus one. Three times I was beaten with rods, once I was stoned, three times I was shipwrecked, I spent a night and a day in the open sea, I have been constantly on the move. I have been in danger from rivers, in danger from bandits, in danger from my own countrymen, in danger from Gentiles; in danger in the city, in danger in the country, in danger at sea; and in danger from false brothers."

Oh, the life experiences that Paul had. But you know what? It's because of those experiences that he was able to minister and save so many different types of people so that "by all possible means" he "might save some" according to 1 Corinthians 9:22.

As long as the gospel is being preached and people are being saved, and the Word is not compromised in any way so as to preach a false gospel, then we can experience the freedom of our faith in Christ—freedom from the world and it's life of sin. In fact, Paul encourages the Colossians in 2:6–8:

"So then, just as you received Christ Jesus as Lord, continue to live in him, rooted and built up in him, strengthened in the faith as you were taught, and overflowing with thankfulness. See to it that no one takes you captive through hollow and deceptive philosophy, which depends on human tradition and the basic principles of this world rather than on Christ."

Notice that Paul instructs them not to be taken captive by hollow and deceptive philosophies and human traditions. There were an awful lot of false teachings perpetuated in Paul's day, which is why he repeatedly tells the Colossians and the Galatians as well not to be deceived by them. There are also a lot of "traditions" that are steeped in the minds of people, saved and unsaved alike, that have no root in scripture whatsoever. So why should we be bound by someone else's idea, for example, of what "Christian music" is supposed to be? Has it ever occurred to anyone that Christian rap and hip-hop movements signify the celebration of freedom from a life of sin? Participants in Christian hip-hop are not preaching a false Gospel, so why not let them experience their true freedom in Christ, represented by the music they perform?

Paul talks in Galatians 5 about not returning to the "yoke of slavery" of the Law because the mistake made by the Galatians was continually trying to be justified by the Law instead of by grace they received through their faith in Christ. By the same token, we cannot be justified by what we think of in our own minds as "right" or "wrong," or by being "for this" and "against that." In fact, this type of thinking can lead to our spiritual destruction. Proverbs 14:12 and

16:25 both echo the same sentiment: "There is a way that seems right to a man, but in the end it leads to death." And Jeremiah 17:5 says, "Cursed is the one who trusts in man, who depends on flesh for his strength and whose heart turns away from the LORD."

In the book of Hebrews, once again, Paul warns Christian Jews who were once orthodox Jews against turning back to their old traditions and putting their faith in the Law. They were under heavy persecution from the Roman government and many were tried and tested to the point of death because their freedom in Christ was under attack.

Our country was founded on Christian principles, as well. Most of our founding fathers were believers. Our currency still says, "In God We Trust." Yet our freedom has come under attack so many times in our history, and since this country was founded on Christian principles, it's actually our freedom in Christ under attack. Remember, even in this country, our battle is always a spiritual one, just as it was for the Jews every time they faced an enemy because the God of the Jews was Yahweh, and the gods of other nations were always demonic. Unfortunately, these gods became a snare to the Jews, who began worshipping them as well. Deuteronomy 32:16-17 says of these gods, "They stirred him to jealousy with strange gods; with abominable practices they provoked him to anger. They sacrificed to demons which were no gods, to gods they had never known." And Psalm 106:35-37 says, "They mingled with the nations and learned to do as they did. They served their idols, which became a snare to them. They sacrificed their sons and their daughters to the demons." The battles the Jews faced, therefore, were as much spiritual as physical.

This same principle holds true even in the United States. September 9, 2001, will always stand as a day that our country's freedom came under attack, and millions of people in this country continue to see that battle as not only a physical fight, but a spiritual battle as well. Even 9/11 aside, Satan is still trying to bind this country that was founded on Jesus Christ. We still fight for the freedom to preserve life, Godly families, Godly marriages, and the purity of our very bodies. Practically speaking, we cannot continue to sacrifice ourselves to demonic idols the way the Jews did; our idols are becoming a snare to us. We know, however, that Satan will ultimately be defeated. In fact he's already been defeated. He was defeated at the cross of Calvary when God paved the way for an even greater freedom than the one offered by this country—freedom in Jesus Christ for those who want to be released from the chains that bind them, whether those chains be legalism, guilt, past mistakes, sin, etc. We were indeed bought with a price, and our Savior paid the price for all of us on the cross, and was raised to new life. That is why John 8:36 says, "If the Son sets you free, you will be free indeed."

Chapter 5
The Right Heart Attitude

W e in the Christian hip hop industry, like millions of other Spirit-filled Christians, know that having a right heart with the Lord is paramount not only in our ministry, but just in our day-to-day Christian walks. Many people don't realize this, but God was more concerned with the heart even in the Old Testament than He was the sacrifices. Lest we forget, the evil in men's hearts was the entire reason for the flood. Genesis 6:5 tells us, "The LORD saw how great man's wickedness on the earth had become, and that every inclination of the thoughts of his heart was only evil all the time."

Needless to say, having an improper heart attitude can

and has put mankind on dangerous grounds. Jesus said three times in Matthew 15:11, Mark 7:15, and Mark 7:20 that it's what comes out of a man that makes him unclean, not what goes into him. In other words, it's what comes out of a man's heart that makes him unclean, not what does into his mouth (i.e. food). Luke 6:45 says, "The good man brings good things out of the good stored up in his heart, and the evil man brings evil things out of the evil stored up in his heart. For out of the overflow of his heart his mouth speaks."

When we speak of Christian hip-hop, we can use the Old Testament Ark of the Covenant to symbolize a person. Just as the Israelites carefully made the Ark, God made people. Just as the Ark was a reminder that God was with them, the Holy Spirit serves as a reminder for us today that God is with us. Just as the Ark moved from one place to another, so do people, as God's messengers. And just like us, what mattered most was what was inside the Ark (i.e. God's Word Aaron's staff as a reminder of the miracles God can and has done, and manna from heaven, or the bread of life for His people), not what was on the outside. And finally, the ark contained two carved cherubim on each side; just like the Ark, we have angels all around us.

But if we were to look at this moving ark as a person, we would see inside are the fulfilled Law of Moses, Jesus Himself, and the Holy Spirit, although we should be warned that just because we may have the Holy Spirit living inside of us, that does not mean that we are controlled by Him. For every time we sin we grieve the Holy Spirit, and every time we don't do what He's leading us to do, we quench His fire. Ephesians 4:30 commands us not to grieve the Holy Spirit, and numerous scriptures indicate that we can actually sabotage our own prayers to the Lord by not having a right heart with God because sin puts a barrier in our fellowship with God. 1 Peter 3:12 says, for example, "For the eyes of the Lord are on the righteous and his ears are attentive to their prayer, but the face of the Lord is against those who do evil." Other references along these same lines include Psalm 66:18, Proverbs 15:29, Proverbs 28:9, Isaiah 1:15, Isaiah 59:2-3, and James 4:3.

For our relationship with Christ to be restored, we must continually carry out 1 John 1:9 on a daily basis: "If we confess our sins, he is faithful and just and will forgive us our sins and purify us from all unrighteousness." Being led by the Holy Spirit means letting God rule our Christian lives. Just as the glory of the Lord was inside a wooden, handmade Ark, Jesus lives inside of us today through the ministry of the Holy Spirit. And just as the Ark represented the presence of God for the Israelites as they moved from one place to another, the Holy Spirit is the presence of God within us. God is just as holy now as He was to the people of Israel. He may manifest Himself in different ways (anyway He chooses, actually), but He never changes. James 1:17 says, "Every good and perfect gift is from above, coming down from the Father of the heavenly lights, who does not change like shifting shadows."

The Ark of the Covenant indeed represented the holiness of God, and God expects us to revere that holiness and respond to it properly. In fact, the only ones who were allowed to move it were the Levites (Deuteronomy 10:8, 31:9, and 31:25). This was God's commandment for how the Ark got from one place to the next. When David brought the Ark to Jerusalem in 2 Samuel 6, he and his men set the Ark on a cart, which was not the proper way to move it. And in verse 6, when Uzzah reached out to steady the cart, God immediately struck him down and he died. Even though David mourned greatly for this man, verse 7 calls Uzzah's act "irreverent" because he didn't have respect for God's holiness and His commands. Case in point: Christian hip-hop artists are very careful to revere God's holiness and perfection and stand in complete awe of it, just like other Spirit-filled Christians. We know fully the seriousness of our walks.

Even though we are sinners, God lives inside each of us as believers, just as He lived inside the Ark. Our flesh and blood cannot enter the kingdom of heaven. We couldn't even approach God directly until the curtain was torn in two after Jesus' crucifixion, which ushered in the New Covenant. It is written in Isaiah 64:6, "All of us have become like one who is unclean, and all our righteous acts are like filthy rags; we all shrivel up ike a leaf, and like the wind our sins sweep us away." And yet, God calls our bodies here in the New Testament "the temples of the Holy Spirit (1 Corinthians 6:19). We are not our own; we were bought with a price, and we as Christian hip-hop artists are very well aware of that.

Case in point: God can do anything, use anything, or anyone for His purpose. He guided the Israelites, He filled Solomon's temple with His glory, and He fills us today. If God can live within us then he can surely use Christian hip hop to lead people to Him. As I've grown in my walk with the Lord, I've become very well aware of how God uses relationships to draw people to Him, and a lot of it involves being around like-minded Christians. We were not meant to be isolated or live life in a vacuum. Adam and Eve was the first human relationship because God said it is good for the man not to be alone. Now this doesn't mean that we were all called to marriage, as I explained in my first book, The Blessed Life of Christian Singles, but it does mean that we were not meant to be islands, all alone without anyone else around.

And Eve was in a sense "like-minded" with Adam because from these two came the entire human race. In fact, Genesis 3:20 calls Eve, "the mother of all the living." In addition, God called her Adam's "helper" in Genesis 2:18. And each of us needs a "helper" around all of us today, whether that helper be a spouse, or simply close Christian friends. Being around like-minded Christians gives us a sense that we have a greater purpose here than just carrying out the day-to-day routine. Fellowship, simply put, is sharing the things of Christ in common with other believers, and I'd highly encourage everyone reading this to do a word study on fellowship so that you have a greater understanding of what it is because many believer don't experience biblical fellowship. They think it's hanging out in front of the TV, or going to a pizza party, when fellowship is a spiritual experience that nonbelievers cannot have because they don't have a personal relationship with Jesus Christ. And it's our relationships with Christ and one another that make fellowship special.

When Adam realized that there was no one else like him, God made him Eve his helper. In a similar way, God can provide helpers for you in ministry, whatever that ministry may be. For us in the Christian hip-hop realm, it's other musicians who share the same love for Christ, for our music, and for relating the message of Christ to other people. And it's all this that we use to produced good fruits for the kingdom of God. And, as discussed previously in this book, we are all held accountable for the resources that God provides for us to carry out our mission of winning souls for Christ.

With all that in mind, what talents, gifts, abilities, other people, and resources has God entrusted you with to accomplish the task He's given you?

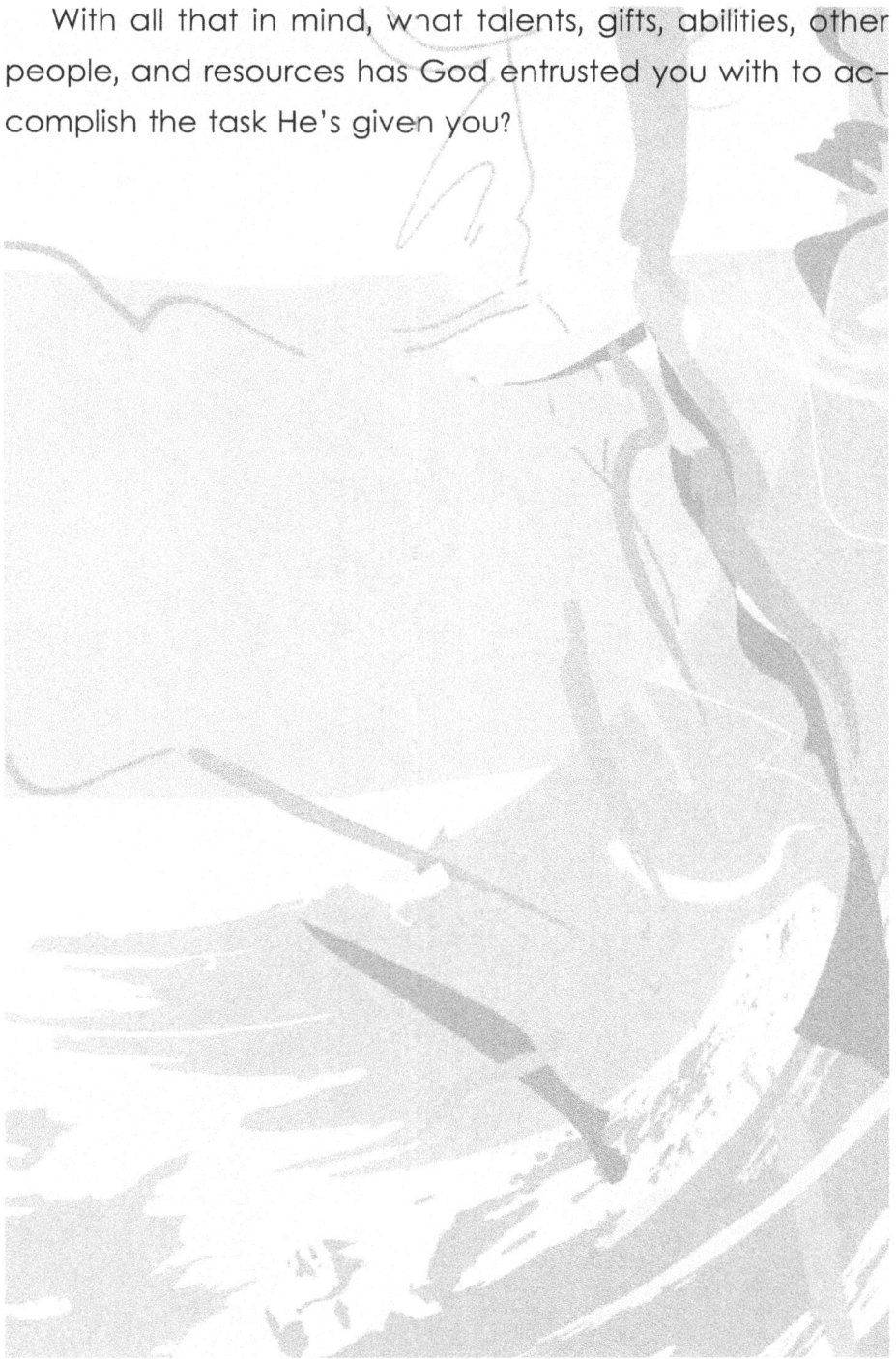

Chapter 6
Christian Hip Hop
Ministries

C hristian hip hop has serviced a lot of areas for the kingdom of God. When I was serving in the U.S. Army in Korea, my brother told me about an internet Christian hip hop show called Holy Cultural Radio, which uses the Word of God combined with the hip-hop style of music to communicate scripture. The first time I listen to that show I was hooked. Being a Christian in the military can be quite challenging if we're not keeping in step with the Holy Spirit. Many times in the military, I was somewhat isolated from a lot of brothers and sisters in Christ, so Holy Cultural Radio kept me on the internet listening to God's Word while I was overseas.

To reach a diverse audience, the radio show featured several other styles of music, which were used in conjunction with God's Word. Being from the East Coast, I enjoyed listening to lyrics set to gritting drum sounds. The show also featured music that would have been received well by the Deep South, the Midwest, and the Pacific regions of the United States. That's what made the show so valuable; it had a styles of music that everyone could relate to.

Christian hip hop comes in many forms that glorify God. http://www.holyhiphop.com is another internet service that benefits the body of Christ. The site features chat rooms where people can post their Christian rap online for public listening. In addition, "holy hip hop" awards programs are held in different cities throughout the United States and abroad where Christians from all walks of life come together and worship God.

Most Christian artists I know are extremely God fearing. My brother Shamel Shiloh, for example, has been performing Christian hip hop for quite some time. His CD, "He Is Alive" has touched so many lives. His shows are largely attended by high school-age kids who come to hear the Word of God preached so that seeds are planted early on in their young lives. Needless to say, his ministry produces an enormous amount of fruit for the kingdom of God.

Hazakim, as another example, is a Jewish rap group for Jesus. They really bring the Word of God forward in a way that immediately jumps out and grabs people's attention. Their first CD is called "Hip Hologetics," which means hip hop in the form of apologetics, which is all about making a defense for the gospel. And that is what this book is all about as well, making a Godly defense the same way the Apostle Paul did in 1 Corinthians 9. He made another defense in Acts 17 by telling the people of Athens who their "unknown god" was. In Acts 17:23, he says, "Now what you worship as something unknown I am going to proclaim to you." That's all Christian hip-hop artists are trying to do as well——make a God who is unknown to many, KNOWN to many!

Jesus even defended His own gospel when He instructed His apostles to protect His sheep from the mouths of wolves in Matthew 7:15, wolves being the false prophets, and the protection being the Word of God. Elijah made a defense for God on Mt. Carmel in 1 Kings 18:16ff when he instructed Ahab to bring 450 prophets of Baal to Mt. Carmel. Each prepared an offering for their god. But when the prophets of Baal called upon their god to consume the offering, nothing happened. But when Elijah prayed in verses 36-37, "O LORD, God of Abraham, Isaac and Israel, let it be known today that you are God in Israel and that I am your servant and have done all these things at your command. Answer me, O LORD, answer me, so these people will know that you, O LORD, are God, and that you are turning their hearts back again," verse 38 says, "Then the fire of the LORD fell and burned up the sacrifice, the wood, the stones and the soil, and also licked up the water in the trench.

In Colossians 3, Paul warns us to set our minds not on earthly things, but on the things of God. Verse 16 in particular tells us to "Let the word of Christ dwell in you richly as you teach and admonish one another with all wisdom, and as you sing psalms, hymns and spiritual songs with gratitude in your hearts to God."

Let us all sing spiritual songs with gratitude in our hearts to the Lord for all the varieties of music we have to praise His holy name today!

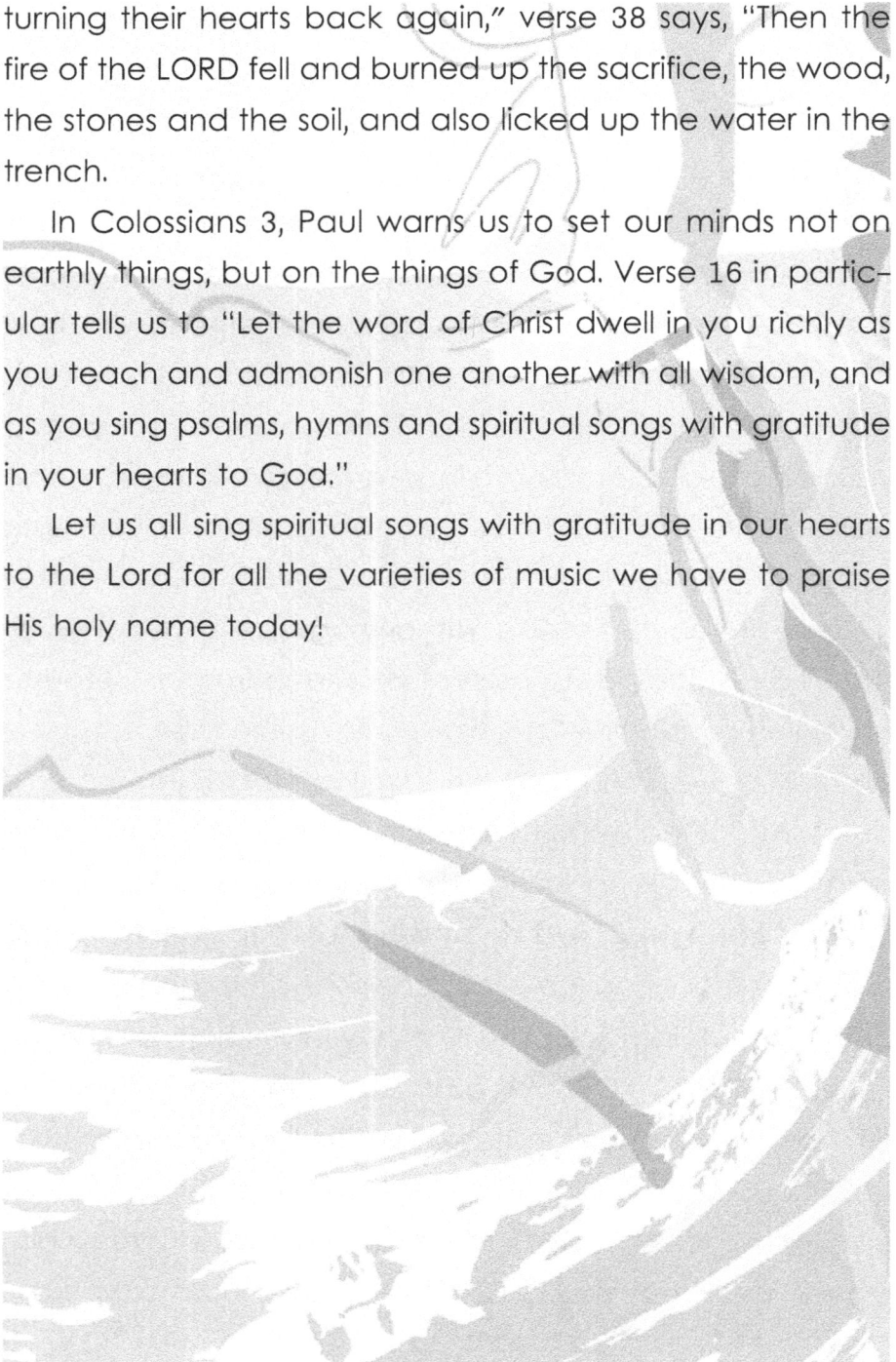

Chapter 7
A New Generation of
Christian Music

T he book of Haggai reminds me a lot of the older generation's attitudes toward Christian music. In Haggai, when the Jews returned from their 70-year captivity, they began rebuilding the temple the Babylonians destroyed because of the Israelites' idolatry. As we've discussed in previous chapters, pretty much all other sins stem from "You shall have no other gods before me" because the god we worship, whether it be the real God or a man-made god, sets the tone and our success (or lack thereof) for the rest of our lives. Worshipping the real God, Yahweh, leads to blessings and prosperity; worshipping false gods leads to destruction, and the Jews have an entire Old Testament history to prove that.

The generation who had seen the splendor of the first temple mourned upon completion of the second because it wasn't as lavish as the first temple. The generation born in exile, who had never seen the first temple, however, rejoiced at the new temple. So, strange, conflicting emotions on the part of the Israelites were heard throughout the land because the older generation was in mourning, while the younger generation was rejoicing since they now had a place to come and worship the one true God.

Today's older generations are not too keen with the younger generations' Christian music. This is nothing new, really. Remember, King Solomon said, "There is nothing new under the sun." If we were all honest with ourselves, we too can remember a time in our once-young lives when our parents didn't like our music either. And I'm sure if our parents were honest with themselves, they, too, would remember when their parents didn't understand their music. So, this is something young people have had to deal with ever since the invention of the radio, and will continually have to deal with until Jesus comes back.

At any rate, the generations who listened to more traditional music commonly ridicule the Christian hip-hop generation just because they were raised differently. Even more traditional black gospel singers like Mahalia Jackson were once considered radical gospel artists because their music was considered too "worldly." Now, however, Jackson is considered the queen of gospel music, and despite what people have said about her, she reached out and touched a lot of lost souls for Christ. Granted, some gospel artists do try to be too much like the world, to the point where universalism or ecumenicalism becomes the central theme, even though that may not be their intent. But preaching the true gospel message is essential to avoid a) judgment and b) leading others astray.

So many have been touched and blessed by Christian hip hop. Danny Rodriguez, also known as D-Boy, used Christian hip hop to preach the gospel and get our youth out of gangs. On October 06, 1990, he was shot and killed, martyred for the gospel. Vanilla Ice not only paid a tribute to him, but called D-Boy his "homie," which means he really touched Ice in a powerful, life-changing way. The people that D-Boy touched may or may not be right with God, but he planted seeds at the very least. Needless to say, his legacy will live on throughout eternity.

Has Jesus laid on your heart a legacy to leave to others? Has He brought people in your life to preach the gospel to? Have you done it? Or have you "boxed God in" because He is leading you to do it in a way that you consider "inappropriate"? If your heart is sincere about preaching the true gospel, it doesn't matter how the gospel is preached. Heck, even if your motives aren't sincere, the gospel will still get out. Remember, Paul said in Philippians 1:18, "But what does it matter? The important thing is that in every way, whether from false motives or true, Christ is preached. And because of this I rejoice."

So, what are you waiting for? Start preaching!

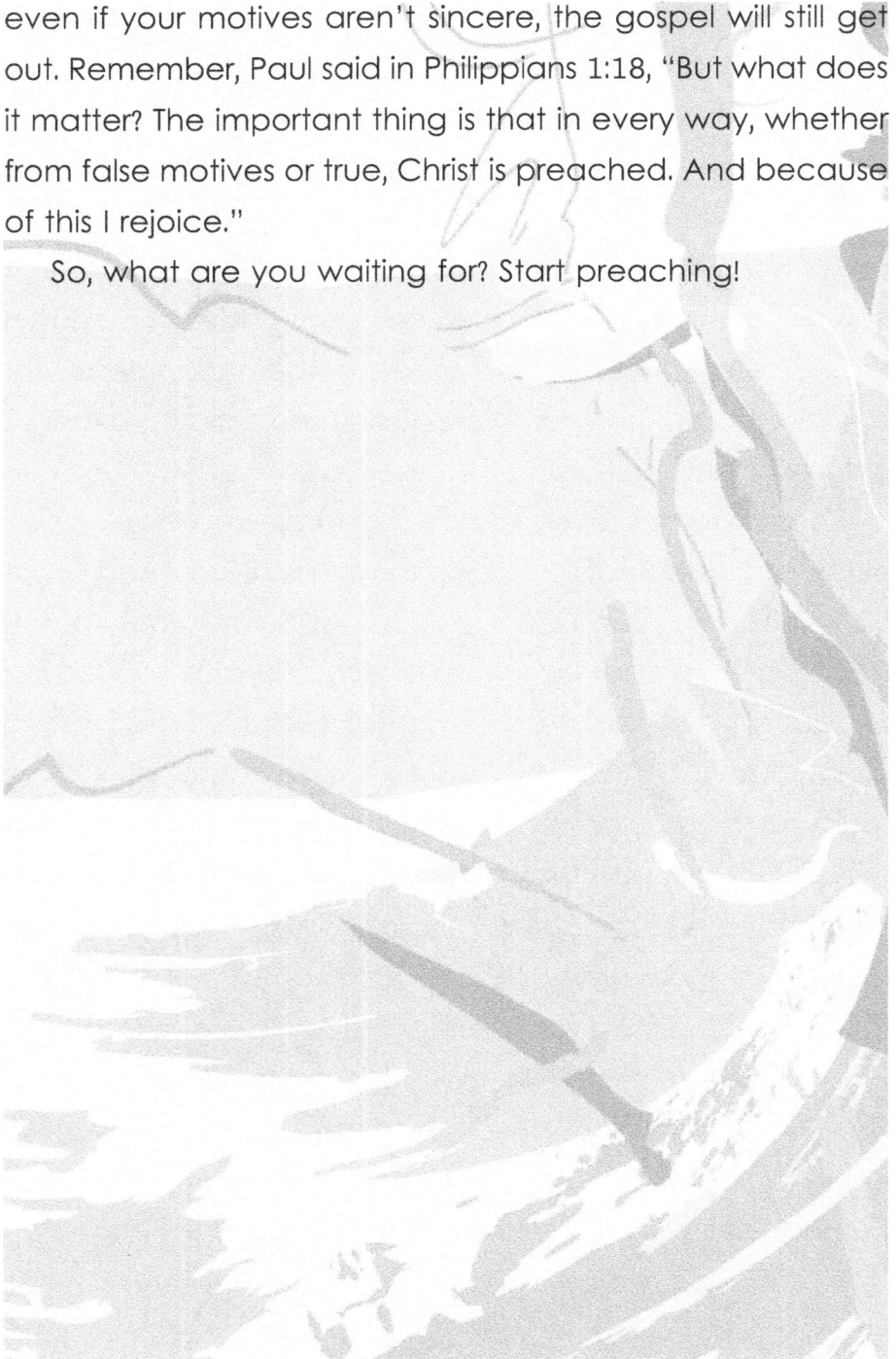

Chapter 8
Dr. Stephen Wiley: The Grandfather of Gospel Rap

D r. Stephen Wiley, born in Tulsa, Oklahoma, became the first artist in music history to have a full-length gospel rap album, and is, in fact considered the "Grandfather of Gospel Rap." His album, released in 1985, was entitled, "Bible Break," and reached #14 on Christian radio in 1986.

Even though he represents Christian rap more than hip hop, in the 1980s, he wholeheartedly believed that the church could use Christian hip hop to have a positive impact on our nation's youth. So, instead of waiting for someone else to begin the trend, he launched several Christian hip hop CDs and became a pioneer in this genre of Christian music.

Initially considered an embarrassment by one CCM reviewer, Dr. Wiley set a Godly precedence for generations to come. And a 1988 edition of Spin magazine named him the "Grandmaster of Rap." Wiley believes that no matter what anyone says or thinks about us, we can never go wrong as long as we are obeying and serving God. In the early 1980s, Dr. Wiley wrote a song for Kurtis Blow that rose to #71 on the Billboard charts. Today, Kurtis Blow is a music pastor and leads a powerful Christian hip hop ministry.

Dr. Wiley later served as an assistant pastor and youth minister at the Crenshaw Christian Center in Los Angeles, under Frederick K.C. Price. He then released two more albums, one of which spawned a song called "Peace," reaching #13 on the Christian charts. The other album, Rhythm and Poetry, made in 1990, released a #14 hit duet with Renee Garcia. In 1991, his song called "Attitude," from the album Rhapsody, hit #14 as well.

Dr. Wiley says that we are all to be fishers of men, just as Jesus commanded. And Dr. Wiley used gospel rap in his life as "bait" to bring in the souls. This is exactly how Christian hip hop is used—as bait for those souls who identify with this style of music. Today Dr. Wiley and his wife Pamela serve as pastors of Praise Center Family Church in Tulsa.

Corey Red is another Christian hip hopper who really ministered to me through his music. Here was a man living on the streets of Bronx, New York, and came literally within an inch of death when a blade nearly pierced his heart. Now he raps for Christ and is one of the most influential Christian hip hop MCs of all time.

I've also personally witnessed how God has transformed my brother Shamel Shiloh's life, inside and out. He raps because his heart is devoted to seeing lives change for Jesus. Back in 1988, when I heard the award-winning song, "It's Time To Make A Change," by Teddy Reliy, I decided I really wanted to rap for Jesus. I said to myself, "If Teddy can do it, so can I." So I wrote my first gospel rap a few months later. It was short, but I was proud of it nonetheless. It goes like this:

"Nothing in the world
can tear me apart
because the Lord Jesus Christ
lives inside of my heart
he died on the cross
for our sins
I will be with him
even to the end."

Who would have known that God would use Teddy Reliy

to make me realize that I can rap, too. Unfortunately, my rap career was always up and down; I never really did anything with it. I rapped a time or two in front of my church, but after examining my efforts, I concluded, "Why keep holding on to rap if I'm not going to do anything with it?" I really enjoy the culture, though, and have always found myself speaking up for Christian hip hop. So, perhaps I missed my "rap calling," but all things work together for good for those who love the Lord (Romans 8:28). I'm very grateful that God has given me a chance to be part of and defend this great Christian hip hop culture in a Christ-like manner. 1 Peter 3:15 says to always be ready to give a reason for the hope that you have. I believe in the Christian hip hop hope because it wins souls for Christ from all walks of life.

I also have to give credit to my mom and dad. Back in 1987, my mom told my brother and I that a Christian rap group was coming to visit the church. She was so inspired by them that she was comparing them to the famous group Run DMC. Needless to say, it was a seed that was planted and grew to great heights. That was the first time I ever heard Christian rap. Now my dad is pastor and a great encourager. He always rooted for us when we did Christian rap or hip hop, as long as we did it for Christ, and I'm very grateful to God that He put me in such a supportive family.

Chapter 9
God Looks At the Heart

S o many people who are against Christian hip hop have what I call "religious fever." They think they will only find God in the piano or the organ or ...dare we say it...gasp!...the acoustic guitar! Fact is, though, God has a way of showing up where we least expect Him, using methods we never thought He would. Why? Because God is sovereign over ALL of His creation, and that means, the traditional and the contemporary, the sinners and the saints, the most beautiful places in the world, and the most shunned.

God can use anything He wants to bring people to Him by any means He chooses. Remember, He used some of the most vile nations in scripture, to minister to, protect, and restore Israel. But as scripture proves in this chapter, even our most "holy" intentions are like filthy rags in God's eyes. So before we can come together and worship God as He is as one body united under Christ, we need to know who we are, and understand that His ways are not our own.

Some of the greatest men in the Bible had a case of religious fever. Such was the case of Peter, as Jesus was washing the disciples' feet in John 13 when he told Jesus in verse 8, ""No,...you shall never wash my feet," to which Jesus responded, "Unless I wash you, you have no part with me." Afterward, Peter declared in verse 9, "Then, Lord,...not just my feet but my hands and my head as well!" because He wanted to be wholly part of Jesus and His plan.

Peter caught religious fever once again when he told Jesus in both Matthew and Mark, "Never, Lord!...This shall never happen to you!" after Jesus explained to the disciples that He must suffer "at the hands of the elders, chief priests and teachers of the law, and that he must be killed and on the third day be raised to life" (Matthew 16:21). In response, however, Jesus rebukes him by saying, "Get behind me, Satan! You are a stumbling block to me; you do not have in mind the things of God, but the things of men" because Satan was working through Peter, offering Him the "kingdom without the cross," like he had done previously in Matthew 4.

In Matthew 4, Satan took Jesus up a high mountain and offered Him the chance to rule over them. At first glance this seems very tempting because by Jesus accepting rule over the world at that point, in theory He would shortcut an otherwise long and painful process of going to the cross, not to mention have the ability to heal all suffering as ruler of the kingdoms that Satan offered Him. The problem was, He would have had to worship Satan in order to make all that happen, to say nothing of the fact that if Jesus had not gone to the cross, He couldn't have died for the sins of the world. So, in effect, Satan offered Jesus the "kingdom without the cross." Jesus, of course, answers the temptation by quoting scripture, "worship the Lord your God and serve Him only." And Satan used this same temptation again as he tried to work through Peter above to keep Jesus from going to the cross, which is why Jesus rebuked him. Peter tried to keep Jesus from going to the cross once again when he cut off the Roman guard's right ear in John 18, to which Jesus replied, "Put your sword away! Shall I not drink the cup the Father has given me?"

Peter was very human in trying to protect his Savior from injury and death. That's just a natural human response when we see someone in trouble. But unfortunately, Peter also proved the truth of Isaiah 64:6, "All of us have become like one who is unclean, and all our righteous acts are like filthy rags; we all shrivel up like a leaf, and like the wind our sins sweep us away." You see, the concept of the Messiah in 1st Century AD was that He would be a great military figure who would swoop down and usher in an earthly kingdom, not of someone who would suffer and die at the hands of men. It just goes to prove that God's ways are very different from man's and it's oh-so important that we are constantly prayerfully trying to understand the scriptures and praying for that discernment. While all of our righteousness is like filthy rags, it's important that we know this in our hearts and examine ourselves before God so that He can make our will align with His.

Samuel got a dose of religious fever when he went looking for the next king of Israel to replace Saul. 1 Samuel 16:6, "Samuel saw Eliab and thought, "Surely the LORD's anointed stands here before the LORD." But the LORD replied, "Do not consider his appearance or his height, for I have rejected him. The LORD does not look at the things man looks at. Man looks at the outward appearance, but the LORD looks at the heart." After receiving the LORD's rebuke and instruction, Samuel watches in verses 8-10 as Jesse passes all of his sons before Samuel, but now Samuel knew the LORD's will; he knew what God was looking for. So in verse 11, he asked Jesse, "Are these all the sons you have?" to which Jesse responds, "There is still the youngest… but he is tending the sheep." So, Samuel told Jesse to send for him, saying, "we will not sit down until he arrives." Verse

12 indicates that David was "ruddy, with a fine appearance and handsome features." And this is the one God had chosen for Samuel to anoint. The point here is that many times we think we know what God's will is only to have God step in and correct our thinking.

Elijah caught religious fever when, running from Jezebel, he said to the LORD in 1 Kings 19:10, "I have been very zealous for the LORD God Almighty. The Israelites have rejected your covenant, broken down your altars, and put your prophets to death with the sword. I am the only one left, and now they are trying to kill me too." Then God instructed him to go stand on a high mountain and wait for the LORD to pass by. I think Elijah expected the LORD to be in the great and powerful wind that tore up the mountain, or in the earthquake, or in the fire because it's just very human to think of an all-powerful God manifesting Himself in an extraordinary, earth-shattering way. But instead, Elijah found in verse 12 that the LORD was in the quiet whisper. Afterward, Elijah pulled his cloak over his face and stood at the mouth of the cave to talk to the LORD who revealed to him that He had 7,000 prophets in reserve. How comforting it must have been for Elijah to know that He was not the only one left like he thought. Like so many other people in the Bible, Elijah discovered that God doesn't always show up the way we think He will...but He will show up if we're looking for Him!

Unfortunately, many others in scripture caught religious fever, but failed to heed God's Word. In 1 Kings 11, Ataliah decided to bring the divided kingdom back together. Seems like a good thing to do, right? But just as Matthew 19:6 and Mark 10:9 say, "what God has joined together, let man not separate," it's safe to say what God has divided, let man not reassemble. God was the one who divided Israel into two kingdoms, and it's up to Him to join it together again. In actuality, Ataliah was a descendent of Jezebel and was actually more wicked. She came one baby short of killing the entire line of David, but God knew prophecy had to be fulfilled. Otherwise, Jesus would have had no earthly royal lineage. So, before Ataliah's death, she ran to the altar of God and refused to come out! The result? She was killed at the very altar she ran to. "Religious fever" can kill us if it's left unchecked by the Holy Spirit.

Look what happened to King Herod, in Acts 12:23. He was struck down by the angel of the LORD for not giving praise to God, and he was eaten by worms and died. Religious fever is cancerous. The cure, however, is Jesus, who dealt with religious fever in Matthew 7 when He instructed the Pharisees to take the log out of their own eyes before correcting others. The Pharisees were very zealous about observing both the written Law as well as the "oral traditions of the elders," in Matthew 15:2.

The problem with the Pharisees was that they took ritual

cleanliness to new boundaries. They were so concerned with remaining clean on the outside that they separated themselves from the very people Jesus ate with and ministered to: tax collectors, sinners, women, and people who had been ritually defiled. And of course, Jesus actually called two tax collectors to be His disciples! Oh perish the thought! Say it isn't so!

Jesus spiritually hit the Pharisees upside the head so to speak in Luke 18:9-14 and 7:36-50 when He let them know that tax collectors and sinners can stand in a right relationship with God before the Pharisees would because people who know they're sinners in their hearts are going to be the ones who will look up to heaven even though they don't feel worthy—even though they know they can only do so because they know Jesus will meet them where they are—something the Pharisees would never do. The upshot to all this is Luke 11:39, when Jesus told them that they may have looked clean on the outside, but they were full of wickedness on the inside.

The moral of the story is that since we know God looks at the heart, we need to be sure our hearts are right before Him before we're spiritually prepared for ministry. Is your heart right before God today? Can you worship with other Christians in Spirit and Truth despite our peripheral differences, or do you have a log in your eye that's separating you from the rest of the body?

Chapter 10
God Uses The
Ordinary for the
Extraordinary

T hroughout scripture, God uses more than 40 authors over 1500 years and 3 continents to demonstrate how He can use anything for His purpose. Even in the Old Testament He spoke a word through Balaam's donkey in Numbers 22, when his own prophet wouldn't even listen to His instructions.

As a result, in verses 22-24, unbeknownst to Balaam, the angel of the LORD stood in the path of the donkey to stop him from going where God didn't want Balaam to go. Verse 24 records that the angel was standing in the "narrow path" between two vineyards; that's where we usually find the LORD, on the narrow path. Matthew 7:12–13 commands, "Enter through the narrow gate. For wide is the gate and broad is the road that leads to destruction, and many enter through it. But small is the gate and narrow the road that leads to life, and only a few find it." God's very specific when He wants us to follow His instructions, but it's only because He wants us to experience the blessings and abundant life He offers us.

Anyway, the first time the donkey veered "off course," after seeing the angel of the LORD with a drawn sword in his hand, Balaam beat her to get her back on the road. Then when she saw the angel in the narrow path between the two walls of the vineyard, the donkey crushed Balaam's foot into one of the walls. So, once again, Balaam beat the poor donkey, until the she just laid down in the middle of the road, unable to go anywhere. Finally, the LORD opened the mouth of the donkey, and she said in verse 30, "Am I not your own donkey, which you have always ridden, to this day? Have I been in the habit of doing this to you?" Only after Balaam answered, "No," did the angel of the LORD open Balaam's eyes to reveal God right in front of him. 1 Corinthians 1:27 tells us that God "chose the foolish things of the world to shame the wise; God chose the weak things of the world to shame the strong." And the moral of the story is if we don't listen to God, He will use a real donkey to show us how much of a spiritual "donkey" we can be.

This is not to ridicule us, but we miss our blessings when our hearts are not right with God, or when we don't obey what He tells us to do. The good news is, though, that He uses the most insignificant things (and animals) to demonstrate His awesome power, and He does all this through us, as lowly and insignificant as we are! God even used a stick to display His power through Moses throughout Exodus. Before God placed that stick in Moses' hands, it was only a stick. But God used it to perform miracles. With it, God enabled him to turn the Nile into blood, and deliver enough plagues on Pharaoh so that he let God's chosen people go. In Numbers, God used Moses' staff to provide water for the Israelites on their journey to the Promised Land. So, God used Moses' staff for His deliverance and provision.

God even used the scarlet cord of a prostitute named Rahab to aid the two spies' escape when they came to spy out the land the LORD was giving them. As a result, Joshua 6:25 records that she even lived safely with the Israelites even though she was not a Jew.

Matthew 4 records that Rahab was the mother of Boaz, who was the father of Obed, who was the father of Jesse, who was the father of King David. Rahab the prostitute was in the royal line of our risen Savior! Who would have ever though that a non-Jewish prostitute would become one of the greatest women of faith in all the Bible? Once again God chose the foolish things of the world to shame the wise.

You know, it's funny. Throughout the New Testament, the Jews were always trying to justify their faith by observing the Law. Many of them thought the Law and their covenant with Yahweh would save them no matter how they behaved. But all they had to do was look at people like Rahab, not to mention Caleb (the only other person to enter the Promised Land with Joshua), and Ruth to know that being "chosen" has nothing to do with bloodline. It has to do with faith and obedience to the LORD.

Many people don't realize this, but Caleb was not an Israelite. Numbers 32:12 as "son of Jephunneh the Kenizzite," which made him a descendent of Esau, father of the Edomites! The only reason He got into the Promised Land is because of God's promise to Abraham way back in Genesis 15:17–20 and because of Numbers 14:24: "But because my servant Caleb has a different spirit and follows me wholeheartedly, I will bring him into the land he went to, and his descendants will inherit it."

As we saw in Chapter 9, David was not even considered for kingship until God told Samuel, "This is the one I've cho-sen." But remember what we discovered? God looks at the heart, not appearance, or age, or anything else. Hebrews 11:6 says that without faith it is impossible to please God.

How easily we forget that the greatest men and women in scripture were discounted by the world.

God even gave Samson the jawbone of a donkey to slay many enemies of Israel. Not spears, javelins, or swords, but the jawbone of a donkey! God even used torn clothing from King Saul as a clear sign that God will rip his kingdom from him.

God uses the absolute worst in people to demonstrate His best. As we saw way back in Chapter 1, God used idol-worshipping, demonic nations to discipline his chosen people. Heck, Mary Magdalene, a woman once inhabited by seven demons, was the first to witness the risen Christ!

And let's not forget the woman in Matthew 9:20, who was perpetually unclean and outcast because of the issue of blood she had for 12 years. But she was desperate enough to push her way up to Jesus and touch His garment. For she knew that if she could only touch His hem, she would be made whole. Folks, that is some kind of faith. The result? Jesus turned to her in verse 22 and told her that her faith had made her whole. And the faith of that one woman who I've only met in writing, who lived more than 2,000 years ago, still inspires me today. She now lives peacefully in heaven forevermore, safe in Jesus' arms.

You know what? Today, Christian hip hop is considered by many to be as foolish as Balaam's donkey. But God still uses donkeys to speak His Word, so I praise God that He made me a donkey! Fact is, Christian hip hop is powerful because God makes it powerful, the same way He made all the great people in the Bible, who were rejected by the world, powerful as well. God uses the foolish things of the world----the regenerated gang members and drug addicts----to pull others out of those same destructive practices into a personal relationship with the source of living water. And as Jesus so often said, "He who has an ear, let him hear."

But let's face it; we're ALL guilty before God of judging people or things He uses because we sit on our heavenly thrones and think, "God can't possibly use THAT!" But do you think that Samuel was shocked when God chose David? How about when that donkey spoke to one of God's own prophets? You know what, though? No one rebuked these men but the LORD Himself, and we need to be careful not to put ourselves in God's shoes or tell Him what He can and cannot use because God will show us differently.

God knows how to correct his leaders when they are in error. He doesn't need our help. Not even the Archangel Michael in the book of Jude brought any accusations against the devil when they fought over Moses' body, but instead said, "The LORD rebuke thee." So let us humbly give praise and thanks to God for all that He has provided us to use for His glory.

Chapter 11
Christian Hip Hop
Around the World

T he debate over Christian hip hop reminds me a lot of the civil rights movement under the church, Dr. Martin Luther King, Jr., and members of the Southern Leadership Conference. On the other hand, the content of secular hip hop music is reminiscent of the struggles that came out of the civil rights movement under the nation of Islam, Malcolm X, the Black Panther party, and many other social groups that contributed to the cause for equality and Justice. In fact, most of the hip hop world clings to black Islam here in the United States, while others cling to the Black Panther party, and many give praises to Malcolm X.

The "roads" these groups and civil rights leaders took politically, socially, and spiritually inspired the secular rappers, with the idea that people who listened to their songs would "fight a similar way" their leaders did, according to the social climax of the day. Chuck D from the rap group Public Enemy once stated while shooting the video, Fight the Power, "the march of sixty-three was non-sense and we ain't going out like that." Whether the crowd believed in their hearts what Chuck D was saying, they were going with the flow nonetheless. The point I am making here is that true freedom and equality can be only found in Jesus Christ.

While the civil rights movement under Dr. King was necessary, so many are trying to find fulfillment in the songs that they write and the things they do in day-to-day living. But Christian hip hop only provides true freedom and equality if we accept the message of the gospel. Secular hip hop artists will often mention Islamic teachings in their rhymes, but when Christian hip hop artists mention Jesus in their rhymes, they back away the very same way they backed away from the civil rights movement.

Back in Dr. King's day, the church was heavily involved in civil rights, and 99 percent of the time when the church is involved in something, whether it be politics, movies, or sports, many noses are turned up. Now that the church is involved in Christian hip hop, many attacks come up against it. But Dr King was a preacher and he understood the ways of Christ. When Jesus was on his way to be crucified, people spit on Him, beat Him, mocked Him, and made Him carry His own cross. Then they pierced His hands and feet, and even after all that, He still asked His Father in heaven to "forgive them for they do not know what they do."

Since the days of Dr. King a lot has changed for the better. But the freedom that we have should be directed at building the kingdom of God. Now that the United States has elected the First African American President, I am pretty sure that someone is going to write a rap song about the first black President and his family. Today Christian hip hop speaks out in the same way Dr. King spoke out in his day. Even though Christian hip hop has a different mission than the civil rights movement, it still has a worldwide voice that carries its message all over the world and changes people's lives for the better.

Just recently, a dispute arose over then-senator Barack Obama listening to Ludacris while was exercising. If President-Elect Obama can listen to Ludacris, I am pretty sure he can start listening to Christian hip hop if he hasn't already. Just think how much further Christian hip hop could go if its Christian message reached our elected government officials the way civil rights did! Many Americans look up to the Obamas, so if people like them started listening to Christian hip hop, just think about the impact that would have on our children! Then the message of Christ would literally trickle down from the White House straight into the hearts of the American people.

Even Koreans have their own version of hip hop. When I was in Iraq, I worked with Iraqis who listened to hip hop artists every day, like "50 cents," and watch movies like Into Deep. They just became immersed in the hip hop culture. Think what would happen if they heard the gospel in Christian hip hop form. They'd latch right onto it, and it might even change their hearts. What a blessing that would be! I even seen Qatar enjoying Christian hip hop, and Muslims are passionate about their beliefs. But because they enjoy hip hop as well, I see it as a chance for the Christian hip hop community to serve the people of Islam with the gospel of Jesus Christ. Even in Israel there are Jewish Christian hip hop groups who preach the gospel to other Jews who do not see Jesus as the true Christ.

The impact of hip hop is worldwide. David Cohen, aka "50 shekels," was inspired by "50 cents" back in 2003, and because of that inspiration, he's now known as the world's most kosher MC. Since then, David has given his life to Christ. Hip hop has left a blazing trail all around the world. While I was working at American University in Washington DC, I was doing a detail in a talent show by the college students, and to my surprise I was amazed at the first time

I heard a female rapper from France rapping in French. She was really good and got a healthy applause. It just goes to show that Christian hip hop is an effective ministry tool for the world at large.

Even Christian hip hop groups from London have made even an impact here in America. My wife used to have a radio spot on WOET called ' Rapping for Christ," which provided exposure to Christian artists and an opportunity for the gospel to be heard through the Christian hip hop message. The internet is another huge avenue for the gospel to make its way through, and my wife stepped out in faith and made this happen. Unfortunately, the show folded, but that doesn't mean it can't be reopened. Only God knows why the show ended, but Christian hip hop is as strong as ever, as it continually grows by the grace of God. If God is willing, the show may reopen, but if not, then God has other plans. The bottom line is both my wife and I have seen Christian hip hop change lives.

God is at work in Christian hip hop and He is using it for his glory. And as long as God uses it to win souls, that's all that matters. Remember, God, not us, is the one who draws all men unto Himself. So many people are making an extra effort to try to bring Christian hip hop to a halt that it makes me realize that if something comes easy and without problems, then it may not be the Lord's work! But when God is working, the devil will rise up and attack, and that's what's happening with Christian hip hop.

Despite the troubles that come our way, we will always be victorious if we allow God to give us victory over all that we do. So the devil is doing his job---so what? The real question is, are we as Christians doing our job? If so, how well are we doing it? How well are you doing your job of reaching souls for Christ today? As Christians, let us all think about how we can do our jobs better.

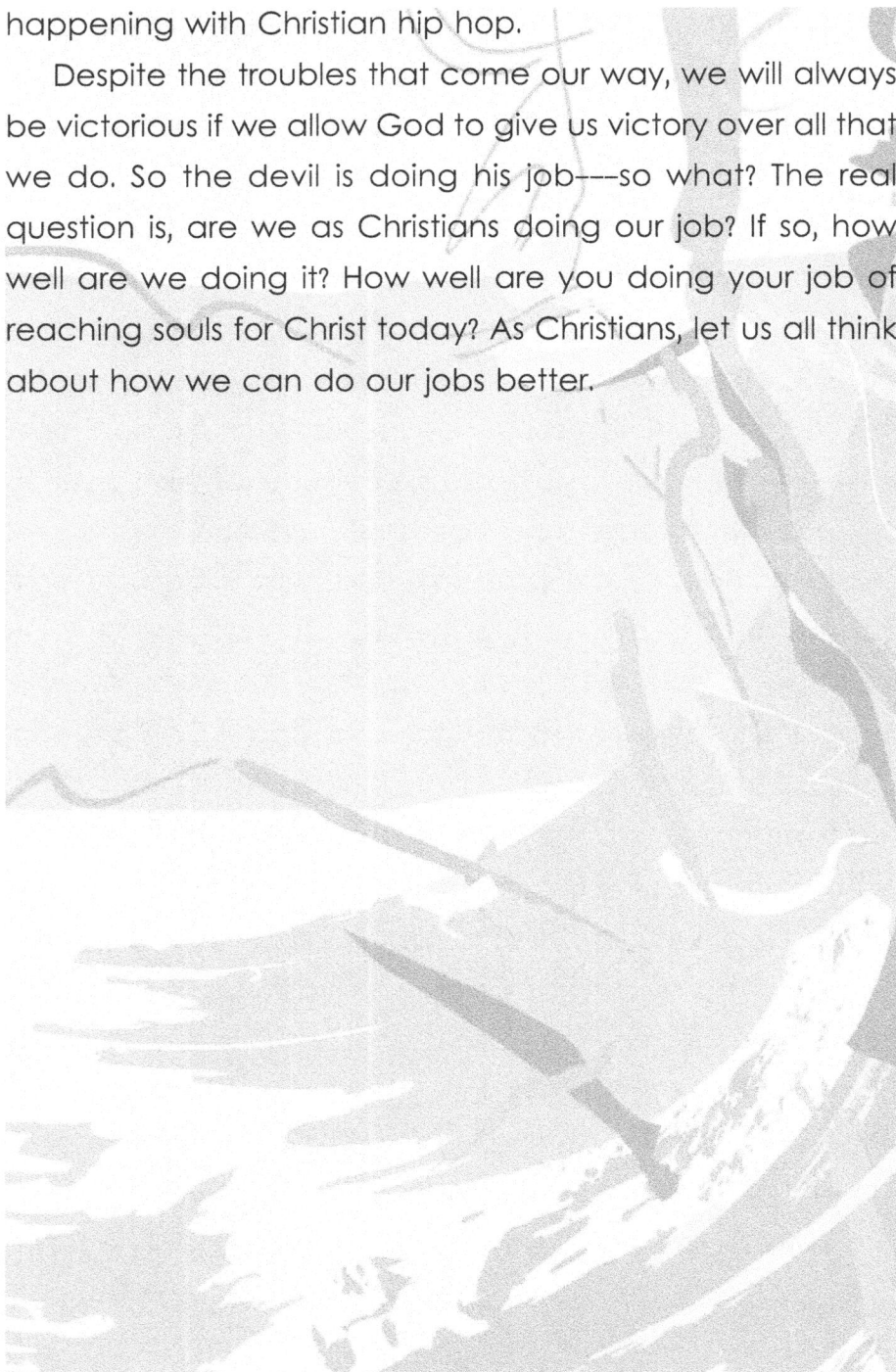

Chapter 12
Too Much of A Good Thing?

Even Christian hip hop can be "too much of a good thing." You may be asking yourself, "How can you overdo the Word of God?" While we can never overdo the Bible, we don't want to hip hop ourselves to the point that we're losing people. Anytime we overdo something, no matter what that "something" is, we can make scripture seem repetitive, ritualistic, and dull. We have to be aware that there is a reason the gospel is called "The Good News." It sets people free from sin and bondage, puts us in a right relationship with Jesus Christ, gives us eternal life (and that life starts here and now, by the way), and changes people's hearts to conform to the will of Jesus Christ. Remember:

John 3:16: "For God so loved the world that he gave his one and only Son, that whoever believes in him shall not perish but have eternal life."

John 5:24: "I tell you the truth, whoever hears my word and believes him who sent me has eternal life and will not be condemned; he has crossed over from death to life."

John 10:10: "I came that they might have life and have it more abundantly."

2 Corinthians 5:17: "Therefore, if anyone is in Christ, he is a new creation; the old has gone, the new has come!"

Galatians 2:20: "I have been crucified with Christ and I no longer live, but Christ lives in me. The life I live in the body, I live by faith in the Son of God, who loved me and gave himself for me."

Ephesians 4:21–23: "Surely you heard of him and were taught in him in accordance with the truth that is in Jesus. You were taught, with regard to your former way of life, to put off your old self, which is being corrupted by its deceitful desires; to be made new in the attitude of your minds."

Now that folks is what I call GOOD NEWS!

Nonetheless, I had to learn early on in my Christian walk that if someone doesn't see my views, I'm not to "beat the person over the head" with them, so to speak. It's the same with the Christian hip hop style of music. The fact is, not everyone likes it, even though it preaches the gospel. But not everyone can relate to that style of music. And yes, there will always be people who will think it's inappropriate Christian music at best and demonic at worst. And there have been so many times in my Christian walk where I've talked my head off to someone, hoping the person would see my point about whatever issue I was arguing.

Quite frankly, not everyone likes the gospel either, no matter how it's presented. But we have to realize that whether someone accepts the gospel is a free will choice, even though we know that no one will enter the kingdom of heaven without accepting Jesus Christ into their lives. Nonetheless, God still uses us to win souls into the kingdom of heaven, so I have to stay in prayer to keep myself mindful of my presentation of the gospel.

The Bible reminds us that anything that causes division in the body of Christ should be left outside the body of Christ. Keep in mind the truths of the following passages:

Romans 16:17: "I urge you, brothers, to watch out for those who cause divisions and put obstacles in your way that are contrary to the teaching you have learned. Keep away from them."

1 Corinthians 1:10: "I appeal to you, brothers, in the name of our Lord Jesus Christ, that all of you agree with one another so that there may be no divisions among you and that you may be perfectly united in mind and thought."

1 Corinthians 12:24-26: "But God has combined the

members of the body and has given greater honor to the parts that lacked it, 25so that there should be no division in the body, but that its parts should have equal concern for each other. 26If one part suffers, every part suffers with it; if one part is honored, every part rejoices with it."

If we allow confusion to come in between the saints of God, how are we going to be effective ministers of the gospel? For that matter, how different are we from the world at that point? We should always be striving for spiritual maturity, and as discussed in previous chapters, a spiritually mature person will always strive to resolve an issue before it becomes unnecessarily inflated.

I have to admit, though, even those of us in the Christian hip hop culture can have tunnel vision to the point where we see everything through the eyes of that culture, especially as African Americans. Let's face it; if our last generation had not decided to fight for justice and equality, we'd be in the position of having to fight "their war" in the present day, not knowing whether we'd ever see the fruits of our labors before we met the risen Lord face to face. Our generation still fights battles of its own, however. We're still fighting to see Christian hip hop being accepted by the majority of Christians, hence the purpose of this book. But remember, God can use anything to reach anyone He wants.

Every generation of the church has its own battles and

its own problems, and especially today, there are so many peripheral issues (i.e., issues that have nothing to do with salvation, such as the style of music we listen to) that separate believers within the body of Christ. But if Christians start trying to break away from one another because of these issues, the body of believers will end up just as scattered as the Jewish nation is today.

The first century church faced many of the same problems we do today (i.e. idolatry, division, false gods/gospels, sexual immorality, unforgiveness, and an unjust government, just to name a few), but the believers seemed to have come together even under some of the most severe persecutions of the Roman Empire. Even Jesus' twelve apostles had different backgrounds, but they knew how to come together in brotherly Christian love as Jesus' teachings enabled them to do so. As the apostle Paul stated in 1 Corinthians 13, if we can't love one another, anything we do means nothing. We could preach Christian hip hop all day long, but without love, it means nothing. Here are some scriptures to keep in mind:

John 13:34–35: "A new command I give you: Love one another. As I have loved you, so you must love one another. By this all men will know that you are my disciples, if you love one another."

Romans 12:10: Be devoted to one another in brotherly love. Honor one another above yourselves.

Galatians 5:13: You, my brothers, were called to be free. But do not use your freedom to indulge the sinful nature ; rather, serve one another in love.

Hebrews 10:24: And let us consider how we may spur one another on toward love and good deeds.

1 Peter 1:22: Now that you have purified yourselves by obeying the truth so that you have sincere love for your brothers, love one another deeply, from the heart.

1 Peter 3:8: Finally, all of you, live in harmony with one another; be sympathetic, love as brothers, be compassionate and humble.

Ephesians 4:2 also tells us to have patience with each other because patience is what true love is. And as long as we stay in God's will, He will always point us in the right direction. Jesus said in John 15:5 that if we abide in Him and He abides in us, we will bear much fruit. But apart from Him, we can do nothing. A well-known old spiritual once said, "God can do anything but fail." He has never failed me, even though I have failed Him many times. But the Good News is if we truly repent, He will forgive us our wrongdoings, according to 1 John 1:9. So, let us worship God in Spirit and in truth according to John 4:24 because that's what God is----Spirit and truth.

Some may ask, "Is there such thing as Christian hip hop worship?" Pastor Rick Warren did a good job in addressing worship in his best-selling book, The Purpose-Driven Life. So

my answer is NO! Most pastors in churches today will an-
nounce at the beginning of every service, "This is our hour
of worship." But that is not exactly true. I agree with Pastor
Warren in that worship is surrender, no matter what we're
doing, as long as we're doing it with a sincere heart toward
God and man.

A Christian hip hop concert with rappers rapping for
Jesus is an act of worship. My writing this book is also an act
of worship. Worship is not limited to one hour in church
every week, or some Christian event that only lasts an
evening. It's total submission to God. Hip hop has a certain
kind of swagger, hand-folding, arm-swinging, and head-
tilting kind of movement. It's a form of expression that
comes from the deepest part of our soul that announces,
"We are free from the bondage of sin because of what
Jesus did on the cross and are now heaven bound!"

Unfortunately, we can be so preoccupied in getting
caught up in the mindless routines of the day-to-day life
and church "rituals," that we are no longer worshipping
God the way we should be. We also have to be careful to
examine ourselves before we worship God to make sure
our hearts are not full of sin. How can we praise God that
way? It's only after we confess our sins that we can worship
Him in the fullest joy. 2 Corinthians 13:5 commands, "Examine yourselves to see whether you are in the faith; test yourselves. Do you not realize that Christ Jesus is in you—unless,

of course, you fail the test?"

Scripture often talks about how thousands upon thousands of angels worship God. But even the worship of the angels is not greater than the worship of man. The twenty-four elders and the beast in heaven worship God, but nowhere does the Bible say that the worship of angels or for that matter the worship of anything else in heaven is greater than man's worship. Even though all sin and fall short of the glory of God (Romans 3:23), we can praise Him in the fact that His infinite grace and mercy still let us worship Him and that our worship is equal to that of the angels and the rest of the heavenly beings! After all, God is no respecter of persons (Acts 10:34).

Let's us not forget that one day we will judge angels when we get to heaven according to 1 Corinthians 6:3. While that does not mean that God loves us more than He does the angels, it is still God's will that we do so. And what we do in God's will is blessed and honored by Him. We are blessed and privileged enough to have the mission of both the angels and the saints.

For those of you who still have doubts that God can use Christian hip hop, I just pray that the Lord will open your heart to understand that Christian hip hop was not meant for everyone, but for those to whom it has been given. Understanding that will enable us to work together as one body without having to deal with peripheral issues, which

Satan uses against us to try to tear the body of Christ apart.

Christian hip hop is a gift from God, and instead of belittling someone else's gift, we should try to understand and appreciate all of the gifts God has given us. Doing so will enable us as brothers and sisters in Christ to love and appreciate one another more fully. As the apostle Paul stated in 1 Corinthians 12, our gifts come from God for the edification of the body. And God enables us to use those gifts based on our faithfulness to Him. Paul didn't mention absolutely every gift that God gives, for His gifts are limitless, but he did say that "whatever you do," do it for the glory of God (1 Corinthians 10:31). Living such a life will only result in God's rewards, even if the world doesn't approve. And this is the attitude of all Christian hip hoppers. We are here to do the work of God, not man.

Keep in mind that Satan will always try to move us out of God's will. He wants to destroy God's creation (namely us) and he would like nothing better than to see us separated from our creator for all eternity. But we know that's not going to happen because we have a personal relationship with Jesus Christ and we have eternal life as a result, as we saw at the beginning of this chapter. And eternal means forever, starting now. Nonetheless, Satan can and does attack the pure knowledge and relationship that we have with Christ and seeks for us to do exactly what Romans 12:2 tells us not to do: conform to the pattern of this world. Only by having the mind of Christ can we test and approve what God's will is----His good, pleasing, and perfect will!

By prayer, fasting, and meditation on God's Word, we can overcome anything, just like Christ did when He was tempted by Satan in the wilderness. John 16:33 tells us that Jesus wants us to have peace, and that He overcame the world. And 1 John 5:5 tells us that only those who know Christ can overcome the world. Who knows? If we stay grounded in God's Word, we may even overcome our hypocrisy that is telling us that God can only use a certain kind of music or a certain kind of worship style to further His kingdom.

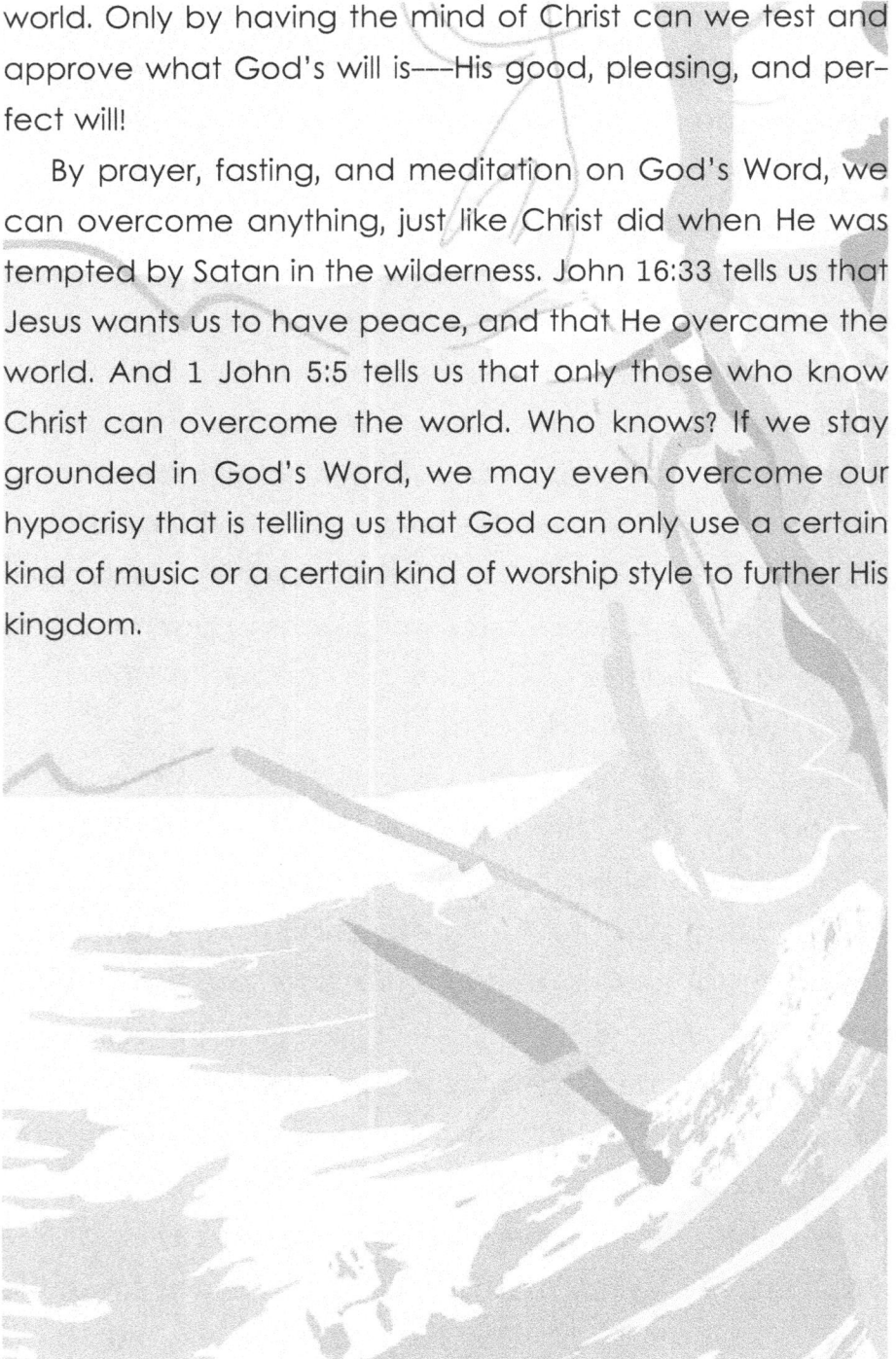

Chapter 13
Christian Hip Hop
at the Altar

Even among those who believe that Christian hip hop comes from the Lord, some still don't believe it's appropriate for a hip hopper to have an altar call during or after a perform-ance. But nowhere in scripture is an altar call forbidden in the church. And remember, a "church" is a body of believers, whether they meet inside the four church walls or a cave in the woods---even Abraham, the father of many nations, had no altar until he built one to sacrifice his son on! Jesus Himself had no church building; He traveled on foot and preached where the Holy Spirit directed. Jesus even said in Matthew 5:20, "Foxes have holes and birds of the air have nests, but the Son of Man has no place to lay his head." Ever been inside a church were everyone looks like they've been cut out of a fashion magazine? Well, I'm here to tell you that John the Baptist dressed in camel's hair and ate bugs off the ground!

The upshot to all this is that how fair is it either to a Christian artist's audience or to the Lord to preach the gospel and then NOT lead them into the salvation that was just preached just because it "wasn't done" the way someone else thinks it should have been done? The only prescription for worship in the Bible is orderly worship, and Paul speaks about this in 1 Corinthians 14 in the context of using spiritual gifts. If you read the chapter, you'll discover that the crux of the passage lies in verse 26: "What then shall we say, brothers? When you come together, everyone has a hymn, or a word of instruction, a revelation, a tongue or an interpretation. All of these must be done for the strengthening of the church." Does a hip hopper preaching the gospel and then leading someone into a personal relationship with Christ strengthen the church? You bet it does!

Matthew 5:6 says, "Blessed are those who hunger and thirst for righteousness, for they will be filled," and this applies to those of us who have been Christian for many years who continually hunger and thirst for God as well as to those who have just come to know the Lord and have received immediate feeding from Him. Fact is, we crave Jesus, the bread of life, every day, no matter where we are in our walks. John 6:33 says, "For the bread of God is he who comes down from heaven and gives life to the world." Even when people called upon the Lord in the Old Testament, the response was immediate. When Abraham was ready to sacrifice Isaac on the altar he'd just built, he knew by faith that God would provide the lamb for the burnt offering. And God did so——immediately——when Abraham saw the ram caught in the thicket.

I also understand the concerns that commonly arise out of a new believer's desire to enter the ministry immediately and use Christian hip hop as their ministry. But remember, folks, what Paul said about the new-believing Thessalonians: "your faith in God has become known everywhere" (1 Thessalonians 1:8). In fact, throughout 1 Thessalonians 1, Paul does nothing but give reasons why their faith is to be praised so highly. Maturity isn't a requirement for leading someone to Christ, although it is a requirement for being an elder of the church——read 1 and 2 Timothy for guidelines on entering full-time pastorship. The concern that Paul had in these pastoral epistles is that a new believer would a) fall during trials and testing and b) be puffed up with pride just like Satan was.

Too many also think we have to be full-time church staff members to share our faith. But quite honestly, God can even use a nonbeliever to lead someone to Christ. After all,

God turned Balaam, a sorcerer with a paid mission to curse Israel, into an oracle to bless Israel instead. A new Christian may not know as much of the Bible as someone who's been growing in the Lord for 20 years, but all a new believer has to do is give his or her testimony of how he or she came into a personal relationship with Jesus Christ. So why can't that new believer bang out some killer gospel hip hop music and then give a testimony in front of the masses and lead the entire audience to Christ? Remember, Jesus is always at the altar, whether that altar is in a church or a hip hop concert in the ghetto.

Some people actually believe that there shouldn't be an altar call at a concert because people had to pay money to get in. How do you think ministries are supported? With money, donations, tithes, and offerings, the same as the church building you worship in every Sunday. And Paul commanded in Acts 9 that those who preach the gospel should earn their living from the gospel. All preachers have a right to expect that God will use people to put food on his table, whether that preacher preaches from the pulpit on Sunday morning, or at a hip hop concert on Friday night. While our ministry, tithes, and offerings belong to the Lord, too many people's idea of ministry is that they don't have to support it because money will rain down out of the sky for the preacher to pay his bills with because He's serving the Lord. But Paul said otherwise in Acts 9, and that's a

chapter everyone needs to read to have the proper per-
spective of full-time ministry.

While there is no mandate in scripture for having an altar
call to begin with, God uses the altar today for repentance,
salvation, declaring church membership, prayer, and a host
of other things. The Old Testament altar was primarily used
for animal sacrifices to the Lord; today in the New Testament, we go to the altar to offer our own bodies as holy
and acceptable sacrifices as our spiritual act of worship
(Romans 12:1). And today, we don't need to offer any more
animal sacrifices because the blood of bulls and goats
could not take away sin (Hebrews 10:4), which is why Jesus
became our sacrifice once for all (Hebrews 7:27). John the
Baptist said in John 1:29, "Look, the Lamb of God, who takes
away the sin of the world!" And in sacrificing Himself, He
tore the curtain between us and His Father in two, from top
to bottom so that through the blood of Jesus Christ alone,
we have direct access to God.

Some church leaders make the altar more important
than it is, however, as if it's the only holy place where Christians can talk to God. Christians, for example, are called to
lift up one another in prayer, per James 5:16: "Therefore
confess your sins to each other and pray for each other so
that you may be healed. The prayer of a righteous man is
powerful and effective." It doesn't make any difference if
that prayer happens at the altar or at the shopping mall.

Righteousness is not affected by where we pray, but rather how we pray---earnestly and with a clear heart not blocked by sin.

So as long as a Christian hip hopper is evangelizing and his or her heart is right before God, He will hear that person and respond. We cannot lean on our own understanding when it comes to the Word of God. Jeremiah 17:9 says, "The heart is deceitful above all things, and desperately wicked: who can know it?" So, our consciences are corrupt and not to be depended upon for understanding.

We also need to be careful of teachers who tell us, "The Lord told me to tell you...." Not that God can't deliver a message through someone else (in fact He does it all the time), but usually someone who believes they have a mes-sage "from the Lord" to deliver is puffed up with pride and may be using God's Word for his or her own purposes. If God is going to speak through someone, most of the time, it's someone who doesn't even know God is using him or her. And Christians are to clothe themselves in the Word of God and sound doctrine, as 1 Timothy 4:13 says: "Till I come, give attendance to reading, to exhortation, to doctrine."

The Word of God has been attacked ever since the first century; this is nothing new. Even King Solomon said way before the New Testament was ever conceived, "There is nothing new under the sun." We haven't invented any new sin, so the attacks against Christianity in the 1st century, are just as prevalent as they are today.

When the Dead Sea Scrolls were discovered in 1947, so many were ready to prove that the scripture we are reading today isn't the text that was originally written down, only to discover that when the scrolls were compared to the Masoretic text, they were virtually identical. The Word of God will always stand and will never go away. Isaiah 40:8 says, "The grass withers and the flowers fall, but the word of our God stands forever."

And it wasn't that long ago, so many skeptics thought Christianity would be "overturned" with the releasing of the DaVinci Code. But Jesus said in Matthew 16:18 that "on this rock I will build my church, and the gates of Hades will not overcome it." And because of this, many skeptics have tried to disprove Christianity only to become Christians in the process. The church cannot and will not be uprooted because it foundation is God.

Fact is, God is using Christian hip hop even at the altar to transform lives for Christ, whether that altar be on the street, your table at home, or your desk at work. 2 Timothy 2:15 says, "Do your best to present yourself to God as one approved, a workman who does not need to be ashamed and who correctly handles the word of truth," and we can do that any altar, anywhere, at any time. And it's important that new believers (and all believers really) grow in the Word of the Lord so that we will not be swayed to and fro like the wind, by every false teaching that comes along.

This is not an easy thing to do, but Jesus said that we are to die to our flesh daily, take up the cross, and follow Him (Luke 9:23). In doing so, we are not to become idle in our walks with God, but rather follow the examples of Jesus Himself who left the splendor of Heaven to come to His fallen creation to reconcile the world unto Himself; His disciples, who left all they had to follow Him; and the renowned faith of the Thessalonian babes in Christ. Christianity is not about sitting still and waiting for Jesus to come back. We have a lot to do between now and then. So, let us not become like those on Mars hill as they sat around listening for the latest teaching of the day.

So, standing at the altar of faith----faith that souls will be won over into the kingdom of God, faith that God will heal the sick and shut in if it be in His will, faith in whatever you pray for as long God approves of it----from the very first altar mentioned in scripture to the one Jesus was crucified on as the Passover Lamb----those are my prayers for the entire body of Christ. So, let's carry out the command of Romans 1:17 and Galatians 3:11: "The righteous will live by faith."

Chapter 14
Bridging the Cultural Gap

Bridging the cultural gap between Christian hip hop and the church can only be done by faith in Jesus Christ. And all of us as Christians should be in one accord because we are all called to be fishers of men. As I've discussed so many times in this book, Christian hip hop is the bait to catch the gangstas and the drug addicts and reel them into Jesus. Remember, Jesus "stood in the gap" for all of us (cf. Ezekiel 22:30) when He died on the cross for the sins of the world so that those who believe in Him should not perish but have eternal life (John 3:16).

So many times we as a body can be so divided over

things that have nothing to do with salvation. As a result, when the world looks at us fussing and debating with one another, it gets "turned off" to Christianity. Many times, however, people living according to the world don't want to believe because they want to keep living according to their sinful desires without being held accountable. Nonetheless, as Christians, if we cannot agree on even relatively minor issues among ourselves, then how can we be a light to a fallen world when the world sees no difference in us?

Bridging the cultural gap means keeping our eyes on Jesus and not on ourselves, our circumstances, our earthly treasures, or whatever else that is all about "me, me, me." In Matthew 14:29–30, when Peter got out of the boat to walk on water to meet Jesus, he began to sink when he realized the wind was blowing. Then he cried out, "Lord, save me!" As Jesus reached out to rescue the sinking Peter, He said, "You of little faith. Why did you doubt?" Ironically, Peter was still in the water when Jesus asked him that question, which Peter never answered. Nonetheless, this is the same question God is asking His church today. And like Peter, the church hasn't answered it.

When we try to approach issues from a mere human understanding, we lack faith and understanding in what God can do. Like Peter, we may start off with good intentions, but stumble, fall, and sometimes, "sink" along the way.

When we see an approach to ministry in the church that we're not familiar with, we immediately try to fit it into our little box of human understanding. And when we can't do that, we start criticizing it, saying, "Oh, God can't use that," instead of stepping out in faith. Acting out in disbelief only reveals our own lack of Godly wisdom. Just because we can't understand something, that doesn't mean it's not from God. Hebrews 11:6 says, "And without faith it is impossible to please God, because anyone who comes to him must believe that he exists and that he rewards those who earnestly seek him."

Fact is, if we applied faith to every issue we faced, we wouldn't have half as many problems in the church today with regard to getting along with one another. We are in such a wonderful position with our Creator because we belong to Jesus and we will enter the kingdom of heaven. We will share in the beauty of the heavenly places together as one body united under Christ. I just pray that all Christians would see that as children of God we are more than conquerors through Him who loved us (Romans 8:37). We are not of this world, but of God's world because positionally Jesus built a bridge between us and God. Let Him build that bridge practically, too. Just because we all come from various backgrounds, that doesn't mean we have to be divided. After all, what does cultural difference have to do with the Word of God?

When everyone in the body is living a Christian life, cultural elements can be brought together in a Christ-like understanding. The words from a well-known Pharisee, who taught Paul in Acts 5:39, echo to this very day: "But if it is from God, you will not be able to stop these men; you will only find yourselves fighting against God." This is true with Christian hip hop as well. So let God be the judge.

I'm not out to try to defend every little detail about how God uses Christian hip hop, but the point is to bring clarity to the Word of God. It's being distorted more and more as we see the end approaching. And if you're not a Christian, then you can't discern God's Word because you don't have His Spirit. God's Word is very clear on that. You can receive His Spirit, however, if you want to, because God loves all and accepts anyone who wants to follow Him. So, why reject such a great love? And as for Christians: if you don't understand or can't tell whether something is from God or not, ask Him! Take it to Him in prayer!

I thank God for Christian hip hop because I am seeing not only the youth come to Christ and stay in church, but the "older set" as well. Bringing sinners into God's family through Christian hip hop reminds me of the account of Jesus going to Matthew's house in Matthew 9:10. While the two were eating together, many tax collectors and "sinners" joined them in sharing their meal. But when the Pharisees saw Jesus eating with those people, they asked Jesus' disciples in verse 11: "Why does your teacher eat with tax collectors and sinners?" Jesus' reply in verse 12 was, "It's not the healthy who need a doctor, but the sick."

Matthew had to be elated for Jesus to come under his roof. And the ones who were trying to convince Jesus that He was wrong to eat with Matthew and the others are the very ones who thought they were the closest to Him. Many churches today want Jesus out of certain activities that they don't consider "correct" or "holy" or "spiritual." But Jesus will eat anywhere He's invited. He'll even eat at your house if you invite Him.

Christian hip hop has a message for the secular hip hop world: Invite Jesus to eat with you and come home to God. You do not have to exist in the pigsty of the gang, drug, and sex-addicted world when you can share in the beauty of an abundant walk with the Lord, free from all the bondage that is binding your soul and oppressing you. God will welcome you into His arms, the same way the father welcomed the prodigal son in Luke 15:11–32. The prodigal's father even ran out to meet the son; he didn't even wait for the son to get to the front door! That's how Jesus is with us. He will come and meet you were you are. You don't have to be "all cleaned up." You can be a tax collector, a sinner, a drug addict, a sex addict, a gangbanger, or what-ever, and Jesus will still meet you where you are. Let Him clean you up!

And if the church isn't ready for people like you, it needs to get ready! The strife between Christian hip hop and the church is nothing more than a misunderstanding that can be resolved through faith for those who desire a resolution. Christian hip hop is for those who would like a deeper and better understanding of how God uses culture and other elements that He chooses to use for His purpose.

Jesus is our bridge that gets us over the troubled waters of life. If you find yourself in troubled waters like Peter did when he took his eyes off Jesus, He'll pull you out of the water if you'll just call on Him. While neither the Christian hip hop world nor I have all the answers, we know the one who does, and we can call upon His name anytime we want, through scripture, prayer, and fasting. In this way, we can be transformed by the renewing of our minds on a daily basis as commanded in Romans 12:2. Then we will be able to test and approve what God's will is––His good, pleasing, and perfect will! When our minds are not renewed daily it is that much easier for the devil to creep into our Christian thoughts and corrupt them.

Many people are against Christian hip hop; they don't believe that it can possibly be from God. Well, all I have to say is that God gave us free will, so who am I to get in the way of their beliefs? But such people should know that God holds us accountable for right and wrong choices, so they need to make sure their choices line up with the Word of

God.

In 1610 King James was the King of England during a time when Christians were being heavily persecuted for their faith. The gospel was spreading like never before thanks to the great contribution of the printing press, which wasn't even 100 years old at the time. A man by the name of William Tyndale became one of the very first mainstream Christians to print the small New Testament Bible that we know today usually distributed by the Gideon group or the military. Soon, so many copies had been distributed that Christians started coming to America for the first time because in those days the government in England could execute anyone who wasn't Catholic. And the greater number of Christians, the greater the hostility became.

Tyndale was eventually captured by the government and sentenced to death for spreading the gospel because people were beginning to see that they were justified by faith and not by works. And once people saw the truth, they started breaking off from the Catholic church of that day. According to tradition the very last words of William Tyndale before his execution were, "Lord, open the eyes of the king of England." One year later, in 1611, King James made a decree that it is good for every Christian to have access to a Bible, and the persecution stopped. God answered Tyndale's prayer and opened up King James' eyes to the truth.

In the Christian hip hop community, persecution is happening even among members of their own body. It may not be on the same level as it was back in those days in England, but it's still persecution. And yet, I continually see people come to Christ, really thirsting to know the Word of God. Christian hip hop is like the printing press of old, just a newer media outlet used to reach the masses just like the printing press was in its day. And through Christian hip hop, many have been freed from the bondage of church legalism. Many have come to know the word of God for themselves, no longer needing to rely on pastors or other church leaders to interpret scripture for them. Now, they can discern the Word for themselves, through the power of the Holy Spirit and make Godly judgments for themselves.

My prayer for Christian hip hop is similar to the prayer Tyndale uttered in the face of his own execution: for God to open up the eyes of those who continue to persecute Christian hip hop. Above all, however, I pray to become more like Jesus in His own last hours before He went to the cross: "not my will, but your will be done" (Luke 22:42).

Chapter 15
Women in Hip Hop

Women in secular hip hop are often seen only in a sexual context. Fact is, in most songs, you'll hear a woman called every name in the book except "child of God." The sad truth is that society seems to be ok with this kind of degradation. Looking at half-naked women in videos, however, gives the hip hop community as a whole a bad rep, and this is what the world is influenced by.

Women may not be held in high regard in the Middle East either, but at least they keep their clothes on, largely because their culture teaches that the covering of clothing brings honor. Back here in America, however, where women are supposed to be freer and treated with more respect, hip hop managed to find a way to make lots of money by prostituting its women in the mainstream. Folks, this mentality is no better than Don Imus calling the Rutgers women's basketball team, "nappy-headed hoes." While so many people of all races were angry with that comment, if the hip hop community is selling out its women, then how can they get mad at Imus for comparing a black woman's hair to a garden tool?

In fact, my wife made a comment not long ago, that it's ok for men to call women mean and nasty names and then to turn around and wish their moms a happy Mother's Day. In fact, James says in James 3:9, "With the tongue we praise our Lord and Father, and with it we curse men, who have been made in God's likeness." Women have been made in God's likeness, too, and we men need to be reminded that we all come from women and should be careful in how we treat women as a whole.

My dad preached a very moving sermon a few years back about when Ruth slept at the feet of Boaz, a sign of faith from Ruth that Boaz would marry her. And he did in fact pledge to marry Ruth when he woke up and saw her there. Then he sent her on her way while it was still night. How many guys today would have preserved Ruth's dignity by sending her away at night? How many would have disgraced her by sending her away in the morning when everyone was awake and rumors could start flying? Boaz protected Ruth's honor.

When Joseph was pledged to marry Mary and found out she had a child that they did not conceive together, he was going to call off the wedding in private. Under the Law, Mary could have been executed for adultery, but Joseph instead wanted to send her away so that no one would know and that she would not be disgraced (let alone killed). I'm sure he was confused. I'm sure he was angry. I'm sure he was hurt when he thought she'd slept with another man. He didn't understand at the time that the child inside her was born of the Holy Spirit Himself. But once the angel revealed the Good News to him in a dream, he stayed the course. Joseph was a good man, not only because he wanted to protect Mary when he thought she'd committed adultery, but he also waited for God to reveal what was going on inside Mary, even though he did-n't understand what God was doing.

Jacob is a great example of how true love will wait. He worked for seven years to marry Rachel, only to have Laban give him Leah instead. But instead of leaving Rachel behind and cutting his losses, he worked for seven more years before he got to marry the true love of his life. And because he waited, he proved he loved Rachel, not by his words but by his actions. More men today need to show their love for women by their actions, not only in their mar-riages, but by showing Godly love and respect to the women they encounter in their daily lives without lusting behind them. Those are the elements of Godly love that we are pushing into the secular hip hop community using Christian hip hop.

While not all in the hip hop community approve of the degradation of women and the name calling, those who don't are, unfortunately, in a minority. Queen Latifa took a stand against this kind of thing not too long ago, which set off a frenzy in the hip hop culture because women FINALLY had someone in the public eye stand up for them and accurately represent the fact that they don't want to take this kind of abuse anymore. I don't blame the folks in the hip hop community, however, because our battles are always spiritual ones, and the problems women experience in hip hop unfortunately stem from what we call "sin." We all have a nature to sin, and we can only be delivered from its power by Jesus Christ.

In Christian hip hop, however, you won't find women selling their bodies, and wearing next to nothing in videos. This is because men in Christian hip hop hold women in a much higher regard than our secular counterparts. In fact, many women in Christian hip hop are faith leaders in their own households, much like Rahab the harlot when she helped the Jews conquer the Promised Land. Not only was Rahab spared, but so was her entire household because she feared God. One woman saved her entire household by her faith! How much more do you think faithful women of God can continue to make a huge difference in the Christian hip hop world?

Hip hop is such an important missions field, and the women are just as effective as the men are in ministry because they help reach the masses with the message of the gospel. Matthew says that in the kingdom of heaven, there will be no male or female. Instead we will be like the angels in one big company. Women in Christian hip hop do not have to look to other women as heroes; they can look at the heroines in the bible who walked upright with God. God used Esther to save her people from annihilation; "in the day when the Judges ruled," Ruth, a Moabitess, turned away from her own people, where by human thought, she would have been better cared for after her husband died, and instead decided to follow Naomi's God, and ended up with a place in divine history in the lineage of Christ! Whether male or female, however, we all need to be looking to the true hero, and that's Jesus Christ, our Savior, Redeemer, Friend, and Lord.

So, in this chapter, I celebrate all the Godly services of Christian women in the Christian hip hop community. One of the very first female mainstream Christian hip hop artists I'd heard of was from the husband and wife rap duo, A1swift. She inspired me tremendously because I'd never heard of a mainstream husband and wife rap duo before. Even though there are a lot of talented mainstream female rappers, they are still very much affected by a male-dominated rap culture and hardly have any say in the industry.

This is where the prayers of Godly women can make all the difference in the world. Mary Magdalene, who had seven demons, was healed by Jesus and became the very first to witness the risen Christ. Women in Christian hip hop who came out of the secular hip hop world can testify to anyone, anywhere about the change in them since coming to know the risen Christ, the same way that Mary did.

The bottom line is that God loves us so much that He doesn't want any of us to be belittled or viewed as sex symbols. What can people who view others this way say possibly teach their sons or daughters about respect? Kids see a lot more truth than we realize. Dr. James Dobson once said that we live in a culture where girls are not valued, and if the men are not submitting themselves to God and leading their families, then where are the family values going to come from?

The Good News is that it's still not too late to repair the damage. The minor prophet Joel said in the Old Testament that God would restore what the locusts have eaten. Women in Christian hip hop have the chance to make a huge impact for ministry by reaching out to other women in the hip hop culture. If you're a Christian woman reading this, and you'd like to get into ministry in the Christian hip hop culture, I would encourage you to fast and pray about your decision, and God will direct you in how to proceed with that goal. Christian hip hop is looking for a few good women, and God will do wonders to use them to fulfill the Great Commission if we only trust Him.

The "Rap-Up"

In conclusion, Christian hip hop is not the new church, but rather the mark of a new generation that has always challenged the status quo of its time. The church has been around for more than 2,000 years and will continue forever. Our goal as Christians is to carry out the Great Commission with agape love and not to debate over "how we get there." The important thing is that we get there.

Unfortunately, we can be so consumed with issues that have nothing to do with Christ. It is then that God shows us that those very things that seem to mean nothing can be used for His purpose. If other people are looking at that same nothing, then God can and will use that same person he delivered from that nothing to help deliver others from their nothing to something that can only be found in Christ. When Paul was on Mars Hill in Acts, the people he was ministering to had a God for everyone, even the unknown God. Pau's message about the unknown God wasn't received very well because the people of his day were content with their regular routine. But the moment they heard the truth, they knew they only needed to be saved by God's grace, a truth that Paul nearly died for.

By itself, the "unknown God" meant nothing, but when the people learned the God they didn't know was actually Jesus Christ, then the unknown God meant everything. The same is true of hip hop. Without Christ it means nothing; with Christ it means everything. So, let's go and carry out the Great Commission together, shall we? In Jesus' name, Amen.